A

HISTORY AND DESCRIPTION

OF

ENGLISH PORCELAIN

A

HISTORY AND DESCRIPTION

OF

ENGLISH PORCELAIN

by

WILLIAM BURTON

With a new Introduction

Republished EP Publishing Limited 1972
First published London, Paris, NewYork & Melbourne 1902

BIBLIOGRAPHIC NOTE

The Plates listed on page x were in colour in the original edition;
in this reprint they are reproduced in black and white.

© 1972 EP Publishing Limited
East Ardsley, Wakefield
Yorkshire, England

ISBN 0 85409 902 6

Please address all enquiries to EP Publishing Ltd.
(address as above)

Printed in Great Britain by
Scolar Press Limited, Menston, Yorkshire

INTRODUCTION

The art of making porcelain reached England late—the earliest dated English pieces being the cream-jugs made at Chelsea, incised with the date 1745—although there had been attempts to introduce the manufacture of porcelain into England before this. From the 1740s onwards factories were set up all over the country in a very short space of time: in London, Bristol, Worcester, Derby, Staffordshire, Lowestoft and Liverpool. All these early factories manufactured a 'soft-paste' or artificial porcelain rather like that made in France, but they were very inventive. Bow porcelain, for instance, contained bone-ash to strengthen it, and at Worcester they made a porcelain which incorporated steatite as an ingredient, yet the factory at Longton Hall in Staffordshire made a glassy-paste throughout its short life. In spite of the introduction of 'hard-paste' or true porcelain at Plymouth, Bristol and later in Staffordshire, there was a rather curious revival of experiments with soft-pastes in the Midlands and Wales in the late eighteenth and early nineteenth centuries, while at the same time the standard English 'bone-china' was being developed in Staffordshire. Stylistically the English porcelains are equally interesting, and while only the products of Chelsea can be said to enjoy a European status, the other British factories adapted Continental and Oriental styles in a very individual and attractive way. Worcester is particularly famous for its fantastic and inventive 'Japan' patterns, Longton Hall for its remarkable early essays in the French style and its adaptations of Italian bronzes, and Derby deserves a high reputation for its contribution to painting on porcelain. For this reason and because the English factories used so many varied materials, English porcelain makes a fascinating study, and has always been very collectable.

Queen Charlotte (1744-1818), wife of George III, owned a considerable quantity of English porcelain and Horace Walpole (1717-1797) is known to have collected Chelsea. The British Museum was acquiring English porcelain in the second half of the eighteenth century, although at that time it was still regarded as common ware, and the modern era of collecting did not really begin until about the middle of the nineteenth century. One of the greatest of the early collectors was Lady Charlotte Schreiber (1827-1895) and she developed her 'China Mania' in about 1865, when amongst 'the ordinary dealers, ignorance was the prevailing characteristic of the period' and any 'person with a very small amount of knowledge could . . . pick . . . up the . . . treasures of to-day for the most trivial sums'—a situation which unfortunately does not exist today! Lady Schreiber's collection is now in the Victoria & Albert Museum, London, and her friend, Sir Wollaston Franks (1826-1897), one of the most remarkable keepers and benefactors of the British Museum, presented his vast collection of English ceramics to that museum in 1887. Besides the growing museum collections, exhibitions did much to stimulate the 'China-Mania'. In 1862, for example, an exhibition of works of art was held at South Kensington which included English pottery and porcelain, and similar ones were held in provincial centres, like the one at Leeds in 1868 which included porcelain from the collections of such great early collectors as William Edkins and Dr. H. W. Diamond. This enthusiasm for collecting English porcelain created a need for general books on the subject, and many were published at the turn of the century—in fact, almost as many as are being produced today. William Burton's *A History and Description of English Porcelain*, first published in 1902, has been thought worthy of reprinting as it was one of the best. Its original publication immediately preceded another but less often consulted general history, M. L. Solon's *A Brief History of Old English Porcelain and its Manufacture* of 1903. Both writers were practising potters, Solon being best known for his introduction of the pâte-sur-pâte technique of decoration onto English porcelain (FIG. 85). Burton was a chemist at Wedgwoods and later a director of Pilkingtons in Lancashire, which became famous for its production of 'art pottery'. Both Solon and Burton were able to give some insight into the problems of porcelain manufacture in the eighteenth and nineteenth centuries, but their chief concern was to present the historical facts and to prune away the myths which had grown up around English porcelain in the nineteenth century. Solon, praising the companion to this book, *A History and Description of English Earthenware and Stoneware* of 1904, said of Burton that he spoke 'with the assurance of a consummate ceramist, gifted with a too practical turn of mind to be easily influenced by the faddism of the collector or the aesthetic disquisitions of the art critic', and Burton tried in his book to give a dispassionate survey of what was then known about English porcelain. Obviously ceramic studies have progressed a great deal since 1902. New documents have been discovered, comparative studies have become more sophisticated and excavations like the recent ones at Chelsea, Worcester, Longton Hall and Newcastle-under-Lyme have in some cases added weight to long-held attributions or in others have completely revised the known history of a factory and its products. In spite of this William Burton's book remains one of the great works in the literature of English ceramics and an important document of Victorian taste.

JULY 1972

A

HISTORY AND DESCRIPTION

OF

ENGLISH PORCELAIN

PLATE I.

Chelsea Statuette.

Schreiber Collection : Victoria and Albert Museum.

(See p. 30.)

A

HISTORY AND DESCRIPTION

OF

ENGLISH PORCELAIN

BY

WILLIAM BURTON, F.C.S.

DIRECTOR OF PILKINGTON'S TILE AND POTTERY CO., AND FORMERLY CHEMIST TO
JOSIAH WEDGWOOD AND SONS

CONTAINING TWENTY-FOUR PLATES IN COLOURS, TOGETHER WITH
ELEVEN PLATES OF MARKS PRINTED IN COLOURS AND GOLD,
AND NUMEROUS ILLUSTRATIONS

CASSELL AND COMPANY, LIMITED
LONDON, PARIS, NEW YORK & MELBOURNE. MCMII

PREFACE.

FOR many years there has been real need of a work on English Porcelain which should occupy the gap between the elaborate monographs of single factories by Binns, Haslem, and Owen, and the admirable but brief general sketch by Professor A. H. Church. The present volume is an attempt to remove this deficiency by giving, on a sufficiently extended scale and with adequate illustration, a connected and comprehensive account of the origin and progress of porcelain making in England. Though the mere fact that the author is a practical potter cannot in itself prove sufficient qualification for such a task, the experience necessarily gained in the daily routine of a factory must be of value in attempting to appraise the work of the potters of past generations. For the first time, at all events, the historical and artistic development of English porcelain is interpreted by the light of technical and scientific knowledge gained in the industry itself; the fruits of years of study of museum collections and documentary and traditional information ripened by still more years of experience in actual manufacture. Having no prejudices in favour of any particular individual or factory it is only natural that my views should not always coincide with those of writers whose work has been conceived in a vein of personal eulogy, which puts impartial criticism out of the question.

Attention may be specially drawn to the illustrations. The newer processes of reproduction enable us to obtain results greatly in advance of the older forms of illustration, and it is not too much to say that the plates of this book reproduce the especial qualities of porcelain colour in a way that would have been impossible only a few years ago. The pieces chosen for representation have as far as possible been selected from the public museums, in order that the student might be able at all times to have access to the actual pieces described and illustrated. The marks again are reproduced from photographs. They are the same size as the originals, and are as near as may be to the actual colour.

While the book is intended primarily for collectors and students, an attempt has been made to treat the subject so as to render the story of English porcelain interesting and clear to the general reader. That such a history should prove of interest to any Englishman can scarcely be doubted, seeing how the industry has grown in a century and a half, from the position of a manufacture imported from abroad, to one where its products are readily imitated by foreign nations for their technical and artistic excellence. During the last few months a competition has been going on among all the leading porcelain factories of Europe, as to which of them should be honoured with the order for the new table service for the White House at Washington. In open competition the order has been secured by the English house of Josiah Wedgwood and Sons. Had it been obtained by one of the great Continental firms it would have furnished another text for those writers and speakers who are so ready to croak about the decadence of British Industry. As it is, probably the only record of the event will be the notice in this preface.

In sending out this volume it is my pleasing but onerous duty to acknowledge how much I owe to a large number of kindly helpers, without whose willing and active co-operation the work would have lacked some of its best features. Mr. C. H. Read, F.S.A., and his assistant, Mr. R. L. Hobson, of the British Museum, have given every facility for the study and reproduction of the specimens in their charge, besides referring me to various sources of information which I might otherwise have overlooked. Mr. A. B. Skinner, of the Victoria and Albert Museum, and his assistants, Mr. Kendrick and Mr. Rackham, have been equally liberal of their knowledge and assistance. Mr. Rackham has spent much time and pains in the selection of the marks for reproduction. Among my friends who are concerned in present-day porcelain works I must mention particularly Mr. R. P. Copeland, of the firm of Copelands, Mr. Bernard Moore, of Longton, Mr. E. P. Evans, of the Worcester Royal Porcelain Company, and Mr. George Randall, of Stoke-on-Trent. My especial thanks, however, are due to two friends, who have laboured for me most heartily at every stage of the work—Mr. E. G. Hawke, who has revised each section of the book as it was written, besides reading the proofs in their turn, and M. L. Solon, the Potter, Artist, and Collector, whose knowledge of the history of pottery is unique, and who has not only freely poured out his stores of information for me, but has read all my proofs with the care of a friend anxious only for my success.

WILLIAM BURTON.

CLIFTON JUNCTION,
MANCHESTER,
October, 1902.

CONTENTS.

LIST OF COLOURED PLATES.

LIST OF BLACK AND WHITE ILLUSTRATIONS.

ENGLISH PORCELAIN.

CHAPTER I.

E UROPEAN potters can claim no share in the invention of porcelain. All the efforts that they made from the sixteenth to
the eighteenth century to produce pottery at once white and
translucent were avowedly in imitation of Chinese originals.
When Chinese porcelain was first imported into Europe by some
of the old trade routes of the Middle Ages—most probably by
the Venetians as early as the twelfth or thirteenth century—
it was immediately recognised as such a unique and precious
substance that myths and legends quite appropriate to its Eastern origin were soon woven about its materials and its qualities.
We read that "it was composed of materials that had lain for
thousands of years buried in the earth," that it "was shaped
from a most rare and precious mineral found only in far Cathay,"
and that "it possessed the miraculous property of protecting
its owner from poison." What seems to us both a far-fetched
and ridiculous story—that a cup of porcelain changed colour
and flew into pieces directly poison was poured into it—was
both widely spread and implicitly believed throughout the
Middle Ages.

That the Venetians, shrewd traders and merchants as they
were, having already brought the art of glass-making to a pitch
of rare perfection, should have been the first to attempt the reproduction of this marvellous substance is in the natural course

B

of things, and there is documentary evidence which goes to show that Venetian alchemists succeeded in producing pieces of translucent pottery from mixtures of glass and clay towards the end of the fifteenth, or at the very commencement of the sixteenth, century. No pieces of their production, whatever may have been its exact nature, or of the porcelain supposed to have been made at Ferrara at a somewhat later period, have yet been recognised among the varied contents of Continental galleries and museums. The first European porcelain of which we have absolute record, in the shape of identified pieces, was produced at Florence, under the patronage of the Medici, towards the end of the sixteenth century, about 1575–1585. The thirty or so known specimens of this production show that at that early date—well within the sixteenth century—a considerable degree of perfection had been attained in the production of an artificial porcelain. The extant pieces show, however, in the most indubitable manner, that the work never really passed beyond the experimental stage. Why it languished, and after a brief period was entirely given up, is unknown ; but probably the difficulties of manufacture, and the consequent cost of the few satisfactory pieces produced, or the whim of its noble patron, caused its speedy abandonment.

So little influence had this Florentine porcelain on the course of events that its very existence had faded out of the minds of men until the researches of Dr. Foresi, of Florence, brought the whole story to light again within the last fifty years. It is, however, interesting to remark, in passing, that this Florentine porcelain was made by mixing together an impure China clay (Terra di Vicenza), a fine white sand, and a considerable proportion of glass. We shall find subsequently that the early English porcelains of Bow and Chelsea were made from materials almost identical in chemical composition and character with those used at Florence about 150 years earlier.

There is a gap of nearly a century between the period of this Florentine porcelain and the next European porcelain of which we have authentic record. During this period the search for porcelain had almost as great a vogue with the alchemists as that for the philosopher's stone, and, no doubt, many an experimenter here and there spent years of labour in the search, with results, perhaps, approaching to success, but of which we have never heard. Mr. Solon has advanced the ingenious theory that the true objective of Palissy's sixteen years of experiment at Saintes was really the production of porcelain, and such a supposition is the only one that can satisfactorily explain his unceasing efforts to reproduce " the cup with white enamel," the sight of which was the starting point of his labours. It is incredible that he should have spent sixteen years in searching for a white enamel for pottery when such a substance had long been in use in Spain, in Italy and Germany, and even in France itself.

In the meantime the growing trade with the East, first in the hands of the Portuguese and then of the Dutch, brought into Europe largely increased quantities of Oriental porcelain, so that towards the end of the seventeenth century, in place of a few priceless pieces in the cabinets of princes of the earth, or princes of the Church, we find that vases, cups, bowls, and dishes of the genuine material had become fairly common articles in the households of the wealthy. Contemporary records abound in references to what is called " Indian Porcelain," a term given in ignorance of its real origin, and merely because the Dutch, the English, and the French India Companies were its importers.

To the French potters of the latter half of the seventeenth century, and not to the alchemists and their patrons, must be given the credit of establishing the first real manufacture of a white and translucent pottery, which, though entirely different in the nature of its materials and the method of its fabrication from Chinese porcelain, was not altogether unworthy of comparison with it. Louis Porterat, " Le Sieur de St. Etienne," in 1673 applied for and obtained the privilege of establishing near Rouen a factory where he intended to make " true Chinese porcelain, of which he had found the secret." It seems, however, that he made little direct use of his discovery at his factory near Rouen, for very few pieces are in existence which can, with any probability, be attributed to that factory. Possibly in emulation of his example, factories appear to have been started at Passy, and afterwards at St. Cloud, and this latter factory, which is claimed by some French writers as the first porcelain manufactory in Europe, rapidly became of importance. It is referred to with high commendation by Dr. Martin Lister in his "Account of a Journey to Paris in the Year 1698," the year in which he accompanied the Duke of Portland on the famous embassy sent to Paris after the Treaty of Ryswick.

Following the lead of St. Cloud, other French porcelain works were established at Chantilly, Mennency, and Vincennes. This latter factory was afterwards removed to Sèvres, where the King of France, after lavishly subsidising it, ultimately became its sole proprietor, and here it was that the French artificial porcelain (composed largely of glass with a small admixture of clay) reached its absolute perfection in the pieces now known as "Vieux Sèvres," which command the enthusiastic admiration of all connoisseurs and collectors.

At the end of the seventeenth century the condition of affairs in Europe was practically this. The alchemists' search for the secret of Chinese porcelain, though prosecuted with the utmost eagerness, had produced no tangible result. Misled by the fanciful legends that had grown up in Italy about the earliest porcelain brought to Europe, and apparently ignoring or disdaining the knowledge common among the potters of their day, they had sought to solve the mystery by fanciful combinations and conjunctions of elements of true alchemical subtlety. If any success had been attained it had no influence on the general course of events. The potters themselves had equally failed to penetrate the real nature of porcelain ; but they were, at least in France, successful in producing a pottery approximating to it in appearance, but of such entirely different nature and composition, that, apart from its methods of fabrication, one would almost hesitate whether to regard it as a porcelain or as a curious form of glass.

Surpassed for a moment, and apparently hopelessly left behind, the alchemist was soon to have his revenge. Johann Friedrich Böttger,* an alchemist, who feared prosecution, it is said, for fraud, fled from Berlin about 1701 and settled in Saxony. Frederick Augustus I., the then Elector of Saxony,† and a great patron of alchemists, sent to enquire if he had discovered the secret of the philosopher's stone, and finally placed him in Tschirnhausen's laboratory in the hope that between them these two adepts might accomplish the dream of all alchemical philosophy—the manufacture of gold. Of course, we need not say now that this search was unsuccessful ; but, in endeavouring to produce crucibles which would stand an intense heat, Böttger produced a dense red stoneware so hard that it would take a fine polish, like red agate, on the lapidary's wheel.

This material (known to this day as Böttger's Red Porcelain) was in no sense of the word a porcelain, but its production so delighted the Elector that for the moment he abandoned the search for gold, and urged Böttger on to attempt the production of a white porcelain like the Chinese. The well-known story of how Böttger succeeded, through the accidental discovery that kaolin, under the name of "Schnorrische Weisse Erde," had been used to powder his court wig, is almost certainly a myth ; but, undoubtedly, between 1710 and 1712 Böttger did succeed in making, for the first time in Europe, a material practically identical with the famous Chinese porcelain, the composition of which had so long baffled the ingenious researches of Europeans. The Elector of Saxony established a factory in the fortress of Meissen in the vicinity of Dresden, and here, with Böttger as director, all the workmen sworn to secrecy, and the works practically a fortress-prison, the first true porcelain of Europe

---

* The name is spelt variously Böttger, Böttcher, and Böttiger.

† Also elected King of Poland with the title of Augustus II. in 1697.

was gradually perfected and brought to the condition of an established manufacture. How the secret was taken by absconding workmen first from one factory and then to another, does not belong to our immediate subject. Suffice it to say that between the year 1712, when the mark of the crossed swords was definitely adopted on the Meissen porcelain, and the year 1750, the famous factories at Vienna, Anspach, Höchst, and Berlin, to mention only the more important, were successively established as a direct outcome of Böttger's success. In connection with the factory at Berlin it may be mentioned that the King of Prussia was so desirous of producing porcelain that he instructed the celebrated chemist, Pott, to determine the nature of the materials used by Böttger. Pott was unable to obtain any satisfactory information respecting the materials used at Meissen, and he is said to have made no fewer than 30,000 experiments in investigating the properties of all the known substances that might be used for such a purpose. Though he does not seem to have succeeded in producing porcelain by these experiments, he laid the foundations of modern chemical knowledge of the behaviour of mineral substances at high temperatures.*

The first quarter of the eighteenth century thus saw the successful establishment of two schools of European porcelain production; the German school making a true porcelain, similar in the composition of its body and glaze to the porcelain of the Chinese, which owes its transparency to natural fusible minerals; the French school producing a highly interesting substitute in the shape of artificial porcelain, which owes its transparency to the large amount of actual glass entering into the composition of the body. These successful factories were only the forerunners of a number of others in almost every European country. Of these, the English factories seem to have been at once the earliest and the most successful, so that in the next chapter we must sketch the story of their rise and progress.

* Roscoe and Schorlemmer, " Treatise on Chemistry," Vol. II., p. 598.

Fig. 1.—" BRITANNIA " WITH
MEDALLION OF GEORGE II.
BOW.

CHAPTER II.

IN the previous chapter the production of porcelain in Europe has been rapidly sketched down to the first quarter of the eighteenth century, and no mention has been made of the labours of any English potters. It is a matter of common knowledge, however, that that famous English pioneer in pottery—Dr. John Dwight, of Fulham—had, long before this time, turned his attention to the question. It has, indeed, been asserted that he was successful in his researches, and he certainly was granted a patent on the 13th April, 1671, for his discovery of " the mistery of transparent earthenware, commonly known by the names of porcelain or china, and of stoneware, vulgarly called Cologne ware." Had the word porcelain been used at this period with any approach to accuracy, one would have said that here was good ground for believing that Dwight had succeeded in producing a porcelain of one kind or the other ; but at this time the word porcelain was used very loosely indeed, and, as has been already mentioned in the previous chapter, the same designation was given thirty years later to Böttger's opaque red stoneware, so that no importance can be attached to the mere use of the name. So far as authentic specimens go, while we have magnificent examples of stoneware of Dwight's production, not a single piece of anything approaching in its nature to porcelain has ever been discovered that could safely be attributed to him. In agreement, therefore, with the best modern authorities, we must regretfully dismiss the idea that Dwight ever made anything that could strictly be described as porcelain. No doubt, like Bernard Palissy, he essayed the task, and, failing in his main object, he yet succeeded in producing a fine and distinguished ware of his own. The story of a porcelain said to have been made by Place, of York, has even less foundation to support it, and it is not until 1716 that we can find even documentary evidence for the production of a substance worthy to be called porcelain in England.

In that year a little Essay was published in London (a reprint seems to have been issued in 1718) " on making China ware in England, as good as ever was brought from India." The process, which is described as " a try'd and infallible one," consists in grinding up broken fragments of Oriental porcelain, and then grinding the finest of these with one-fourth part of their weight of quicklime dissolved in gum-water. It is further specified that the quicklime is not to be of the common kind, but is to be obtained by calcining clean oyster shells. There is no doubt that true porcelain could be made by such a roundabout method ; indeed, the mixture would closely approximate in composition to some of the ordinary kinds of Japanese porcelain. The use of gum water was universal among the makers of glassy porcelain, as it imparted a certain amount of plasticity to the mixture, which the small quantity of clay could not supply.

One would expect to find that articles made by such a process as this would show, when fractured, a roughish body of granular and uneven texture, and probably speckled throughout with black or blue specks due to the colours used on the original decorated porcelain. No specimens of such wares are definitely known, but an examination of many pieces, said to belong to the early days of the Bow factory, reveals quite a fair percentage that might have been made in this way.

The late Sir A. W. Franks first drew attention to a passage in Robert Dossie's " Handmaid of the Arts," published in 1764, in which that writer says that he " has seen at a factory near London eleven mills at work grinding pieces of the Eastern china . . . . the ware was grey, full of flaws and bubbles, and from

PLATE II.

Bow Mug.   Chelsea Plate.   Worcester Mug.

PAINTED WITH CHINESE PATTERNS IN UNDERGLAZE BLUE.

Victoria and Albert Museum.

(*See p. 26.*)

want of due tenacity in the paste wrought in a heavy and clumsy manner." With regard to this description, which seems singularly belated,* it may be remarked that while the " grey paste, full of flaws and bubbles," is undoubtedly a true description of the ware that would be produced by such a method of working, the tenacity of the paste could have been little inferior to that of many other kinds of porcelain in common use, for such tenacity as most of them possessed was entirely due to the addition of gum-water. Any extra clumsiness of the pieces must have been due to the want of experience in the potters who shaped them.

There can be little doubt after this evidence that experiments in porcelain making were carried on in the neighbourhood of London after the singular method above described. It is possible, even probable, that the early factories at Limehouse and Greenwich, of which we have tantalising mention by several contemporary writers but no positive information whatever, may have been attempting to work this process. This is, however, pure speculation, and we only reach solid ground with the granting of a patent to Heylin and Frye in 1744, which is commonly supposed to mark the commencement of the Bow factory; and with the existence of undecorated white pieces marked with an inscribed triangle and the legend, " Chelsea, 1745." These latter pieces are of such excellent quality that it cannot be supposed they are first productions ; at least, if they are the first productions of Chelsea they must have been made by someone who possessed considerable knowledge of the making of glassy porcelain, for they absolutely resemble the artificial glassy porcelains of Chantilly and Vincennes. We have seen that the secret of true porcelain was carried from Dresden to many towns in the German Empire, and it seems equally possible that some workman, or workmen, from the French factories may have brought over here the knowledge of artificial glassy porcelain. It is difficult otherwise to account for the fact that within the ten years, 1745–1755, we have porcelain factories established at Chelsea, Bow, Derby, Worcester,

* It is, for instance, forty-eight years later than the Essay previously mentioned.

and Longton Hall. It is unreasonable to suppose that all these factories were established as the result of independent discovery in each of those places; besides, there is too great resemblance in the body and glaze of the early productions of these factories to admit of an independent origin for all of them. The early pieces, such as the goat and bee cream-jug and the crawfish salts of Chelsea, the inkstands marked New Canton and other early Bow pieces, and the Longton Hall pieces, are so obviously alike in quality that they seem to proclaim their common origin. It may be suggested that this origin would be found in the Heylin and Frye's patent of 1744 already alluded to, but that patent is not worth the paper on which it was written.* The particulars given are purposely vague, but the glass or frit is a pure alkaline glass, which when ground in water produces a soluble glass. This, when mixed with china clay, instead of producing a plastic working mass, sets almost like cement, and could never have been fashioned into shape by any ordinary pottery method, and the description of the mixtures suggests that the patentees were anxious to protect the use of substances of which they had no practical experience. Compare, for instance, the mixtures proposed in this Heylin and Frye's patent of 1744–1745 with the mixtures actually used at Sèvres :—

HEYLIN AND FRYE'S PATENT.	SÈVRES.†
Frit.	*Frit.*
50 parts Potash ⎫ fused together.	Sand　60 parts ⎫
50 parts Sand ⎭	Nitre　22　,,
Body.	Salt　7·2 ,, ⎬ fused together.
50 parts of above glassy frit.	Soda　3·6 ,,
50 parts of Unaker (china clay), varied to	Alum　3·6 ,,
20 parts frit.	Gypsum 3·6 ,, ⎭
80 parts Unaker	*Body.*
	75 parts of above glassy frit.
	17　,,　of chalk
	8　,,　of calcareous clay.

Not only were the proportions of Heylin and Frye entirely wrong, but their frit was useless for its supposed purpose.

* Exhaustive experiments have convinced the author that no porcelain could have been made of the materials and in the manner specified in this patent.

† Brongniart, "Traité des Arts Céramiques," Vol. II., p. 460. Edition 1877.

Setting aside any question of Heylin and Frye's patent, it must be said that all these early porcelains were undoubtedly made by mixing a large amount of glass with a small amount of white clay, for they have the mellow rich quality characteristic of such mixtures, whether made at St. Cloud, Chantilly, Sèvres, Doccia, or at the eighteenth century English factories already named. In the next chapter will be found a technical description of the various kinds of porcelain, so that it is sufficient to state here that such mixtures of glass and clay presented many difficulties in making, and particularly in firing. The French porcelain works were, indeed, only able to live on the support accorded by the great nobles, Princes of the Royal blood, or the King himself, and it is not, therefore, surprising to find that the English porcelain factories mentioned, either came to grief in their efforts to produce glassy porcelains of the type with which they started, or found a solution of their difficulties by producing mixtures that were much more manageable in working and in firing. The history of the eighteenth century china factories of England is, indeed, the history of these attempts to produce a porcelain which should unite some of the excellences of both the German and the French porcelain.

In 1755 practically all the porcelains made in England were of the French type pure and simple. By 1760 considerable modifications had been introduced in the paste; at some factories bone-ash was now used in varying proportions, but probably only tentatively; while soapstone was largely used at Worcester and to a minor extent elsewhere.

From 1768 to 1781 a true porcelain, resembling the Chinese in its materials, was produced at Plymouth and at Bristol, following on Cookworthy's discovery of china clay and china stone in Cornwall; but, interesting as these attempts to manufacture true porcelain were, they had no direct influence on the general tendency of English porcelain making. By the end of the eighteenth century the battle had been fought out, glassy mixtures and true porcelain mixtures were both abandoned, and English bone-porcelain, as we now know it, was firmly established. Flickering efforts to revive glassy porcelains were made during the first half of the nineteenth century by Billingsley at Pinxton, Nantgarw, and Swansea, and by Randall at Madeley; but they led to no permanent success. From every point of view, therefore, the English porcelains of the eighteenth century are those which have the greatest interest for us, representing, as they do, the efforts of an artistic manufacture in its early stages, when all the technical processes were in a condition of development and change. During this period, by the labours of men who are mostly unknown to us, knowledge was slowly, but surely, gained and disseminated from factory to factory. Chelsea, Bow, Plymouth, and Bristol successively disappeared from the scene, and Worcester, Derby, the Staffordshire factories, and Coalport entered on the nineteenth century with settled methods and organised businesses. In these factories, for nearly half a century, the making of porcelain was practically concentrated. The bodies and glazes, the painting and gilding— all that can be called workmanship in the narrow sense—were admirable in a careful mechanical way. Taste and artistic skill of any high order were absolutely lacking, and the productions of the half century 1800–1850 fail to warm us with the slightest glow of enthusiasm. Following on the Exhibition of 1851 there came renewed effort, and a period of revival was reached, which has endured to the present time. The methods and the results of these latest factories form, however, a complete contrast to those of the eighteenth century, and must be regarded from a very different standpoint. In the first period the whole art and craft of English porcelain are so evidently " in the making " that one is often delighted by the *naïveté* of the early potters and pot-painters. This charm of freshness and of effort is, indeed, the quality that recommends the early work, and for it one is prepared to overlook certain deficiencies of craftsmanship. In the later factories not only have the pottery processes been reduced to order and system, but the general advance of knowledge has brought

Fig. 2.—BOCAGE CANDLESTICK.
"THE VAIN JACKDAW."
CHELSEA.

within the reach of potters the materials and artistic methods of the whole world. The modern potter needs no longer to fumble after a knowledge of Chinese, Japanese, or Continental methods and materials, as his predecessor did, and the pieces produced by Mintons and Copelands in the manner of " Vieux Sèvres," and by Worcester in the manner of Japanese and Persian pieces, are entirely different in style and method from the copies of similar pieces made in the eighteenth century. The modern pot-painter and modeller is now, in many cases, a trained artist, whose signature is proudly appended to his work, a condition in the greatest contrast to that of his predecessor a century or more ago.

The productions of the earlier factories will be described in considerable detail, not only because they are of the greatest interest to the collector, but also because they represent a completed movement about which our judgment is mature. The productions of the last fifty years can only be briefly sketched, taking the firms already mentioned as typical of the best modern effort, as the movement they represent is still in process of development, and collectors have hardly commenced to interest themselves definitely in its doings.

CHAPTER III.

I⊤ will have been noticed that in the previous chapters Chinese porcelain has been referred to as " true " porcelain, while the results of the early efforts in Italy, France, and England have been described as " artificial " porcelain. Apart altogether from the fact that Chinese porcelain is the first substance of its kind of which we have any knowledge, and that all the European attempts to produce porcelain were in avowed imitation of it, there is all-sufficient reason for this distinction in that the first is a most highly developed form of true pottery ware, having clay and clay-forming minerals as its principal constituents, while the second should rather be described as a curious hybrid substance in which glass has been rendered milky white, partly opaque, and of sluggish fluidity at high temperatures, by the addition of a small proportion of white clay. The differences between these substances—both known as porcelain—are so fundamental that they extend not merely to the materials entering into their composition, but also to the methods used in the fabrication, and particularly in the firing, of the ware. The final products too are readily distinguishable, and lend themselves to different styles of decoration. It is, therefore, of the utmost importance to form a clear idea at the outset of what is meant by " true " and " artificial " porcelains.

In true porcelain the clay mass, or paste, from which the pieces are shaped is practically a mixture of two minerals, known to the Chinese as petuntse and kaolin. The former of these, petuntse—or, in English, " china stone "—is a hard, rocky substance, in which a large proportion of felspar crystals is found embedded in glassy quartz. It forms, therefore, a mineral mixture of somewhat variable composition, which, when finely powdered and exposed to the heat of a porcelain furnace, melts down to a glassy mass, transparent in thin layers, but beautifully milk-white in thicker pieces. It is the vitrification of this natural material (petuntse) in the firing that gives to true porcelain its translucence and its hardness. The other substance—kaolin, or china clay, as it is now commonly called—is a very pure clay which has generally been produced by the gradual decomposition of the rocky petuntse. The slow, long-continued action of the carbonic acid and moisture of air and rain gradually decomposes the felspar of the petuntse, leaving a coarse, friable mass, consisting of china clay mixed with the undecomposed fragments of the original rock. When this coarse powder is thrown into water, the rocky particles settle rapidly to the bottom, leaving the kaolin or china clay in suspension. The milky fluid thus produced can then be drawn off; by long standing the kaolin settles out, and, after drying, is left as a pure white clay, which differs from the original rock in being practically infusible at the highest temperature of the porcelain furnace. Not the least interesting point, therefore, in connection with true porcelain is this fact, that the petuntse, or fusible material, is really the mother-rock from which the kaolin, or china clay, has been formed by sub-aërial decomposition. The kaolin gives plasticity to the mixture, and enables the pieces to retain their shape in firing. The petuntse fuses, giving translucence to the ware, and, binding together the particles of kaolin, forms the whole into a solid durable substance.

It has been generally stated that the discovery of kaolin was the one thing needed to enable European potters to produce true porcelain. On the contrary, kaolin had long been used in Europe, and what was needed was the recognition of the fact, so well known to the Chinese, that two allied minerals were to be found in association in nature, which, when mixed in different proportions, would form both the body and the glaze of porcelain, without the addition of any other ingredient.

Here lies the true merit of Böttger's discovery, surely one of the most remarkable in the whole history of applied art ; all the more remarkable, too, because nothing in the previous experience of European potters could have prepared him for it. The European potters' methods for the production of the various forms of pottery they had evolved comprised little more than the baking of the clays of any particular locality, and the coating of the fired pieces with a thin layer of powdered glass, which was subsequently melted at a lower temperature. It is not surprising, therefore, that when they were confronted with this new substance—porcelain—two centuries of effort were only, to re-apply the words of Palissy, " like groping in the dark." The translucence of porcelain must have been stranger to them than its whiteness, and they naturally turned to the transparent substance they knew most about— glass—and strove to hit the just proportion in which they could mix infusible white earth with glass so as to produce a mass of such a nature that vessels made from it could be fired up to a translucent condition, without sinking bodily out of the shape that had been given to them. The substance obtained in this way was a most interesting and beautiful product, but it was not the porcelain of the Chinese.

All efforts to produce true porcelain were bound to fail until the associated minerals, similar to those used by the Chinese them- selves, had been discovered. In France, for instance, twenty years after Böttger's production of true porcelain at Dresden, the chemist Réaumur, although he had been provided with an account of the Chinese processes, and with actual samples of Chinese kaolin and petuntse by the Jesuit missionary, Père d'Entrecolles, was unable to produce anything but an opaque glass, because no one knew of the existence of similar minerals in France. In England, again, though china clay was known at least as early as 1744, it was only when Cookworthy discovered both china clay and china stone together in Cornwall, in 1768, that any true porcelain was made here.

The primary difference, therefore, between the Chinese and

PLATE III.

Derby-Chelsea Vase in the Sèvres Style.

Jones Bequest: Victoria and Albert Museum.

(*See p.* 55.)

Dresden porcelains on the one hand, and the early French and English porcelains on the other, lies in the nature of the paste or clay mixture from which the articles are shaped. In one the fusible ingredient is a natural rock, and a considerable proportion of china clay is added to it; in the other, the fusible material is an artificial substance—glass—and only a small proportion of clay can be added to it. But the difference does not end here. In true porcelain the glaze often consists of nothing more than the fusible constituent of the body—the petuntse—and the body and glaze are fired at one operation, so that the glaze receives the highest fire ever given to the ware. In artificial porcelain, on the other hand, the mixture of glass (or frit, as it is commonly called) and clay, after being shaped to the required form, is just fired to as high a temperature as it will endure without sinking out of shape, and then the glaze, which is a fusible glass generally rich in lead, is melted upon this body at a lower temperature. The temperature required to produce true porcelain is very high, being at least 1,350° C. to 1,450° C.; while the artificial glassy porcelains were fired in their first stage at a temperature of about 1,100° C. to 1,150° C., and the glaze at a lower temperature still, probably not exceeding 1,000° C.

It has been generally assumed that because true porcelain was fired at a higher temperature it must have been more difficult to manufacture. On the contrary, there can be little doubt that the glassy porcelain was much more difficult and uncertain in production, for such a large proportion of glass was used in the paste, to give the required translucence, that the range of temperatures between the point at which the articles would become translucent and retain their shape, and that at which they would soften and go out of shape, was very limited. The success of all pottery operations on a large scale depends on there being a fairly wide range of temperatures within which the articles can be efficiently produced; so that with glassy porcelains the proportion of spoilt pieces must have been very large. It is for this reason that glassy porcelains were only made for about a century. In France,

C

where the first real success in their production was reached, they were replaced by true porcelain as soon as the essential materials were discovered there ; and in England the glassy porcelains were almost entirely superseded within fifty years of their introduction, many of them indeed much earlier, by more manageable mixtures.

In England, however, the development of porcelain proceeded on lines totally different from those followed elsewhere. The early English porcelains were all of the glassy type, but at the principal factories experiments were continually being made to introduce fresh materials, and to simplify the methods in use. In every case the potters' first efforts were directed toward making the frit, or special glass used in the body, less fluid, and therefore less liable to run out of shape with a slight difference of temperature at the critical stage of the firing. Several mixtures were devised for this purpose. At Worcester soapstone or steatite was used in the fabrication of the ware, with the result that a porcelain which often resembled " true " porcelain in appearance was produced. At other factories, notably at Bow and Chelsea in the later years of those factories, varying amounts of bone-ash were added to the glassy mixture, with the same result. Down to the end of the eighteenth century, however, the custom of making a frit or glass seems to have continued, even when some proportion of bone-ash was used. Pottery making has always been a business in which traditional methods died hard, and tradition in this case was too strong for such a radical innovation as the making of a porcelain body without the use of a frit.

Professor Church has proved by numerous analyses that the use of bone-ash in the body of English porcelains was very widespread between 1760 and 1800, and various receipts for porcelain making are given by him which show that the knowledge of this new material was becoming quite common. The idea that Spode first introduced bone-ash into the body of English china about the year 1800 is absolutely untenable ; but it is extremely probable that the tradition arose because he first abandoned the practice of calcining or fritting the bone-ash with some of the other ingredients, and used the simple mixture of bone-ash, petuntse, and china clay, which, since his day, has formed the typical body of English porcelain. This paste may be taken as consisting essentially of 6 parts of bone-ash, 4 parts of china stone (petuntse), and 3½ parts of china clay (kaolin) finely ground and mixed together. So far as composition goes, it is to all intents and purposes the body of true porcelain with a large proportion of added bone-ash. Here, however, all resemblance to true porcelain ends. The pieces are first fired to a temperature of about 1,200° C. to 1,250° C., at which temperature they become beautifully white and translucent. The glaze, which is also of the same type as the glaze of hard porcelain, consisting essentially of petuntse or felspar, and china clay, but rendered more easily fusible by the addition of boracic acid, alkalies, and oxide of lead, is subsequently fired on the biscuit body at a lower temperature.

To sum up this portion of the subject we may tabulate the materials and methods of the three main species of porcelain thus :—

True porcelain (Chinese, Dresden, Bristol, etc.).

Body, or paste : petuntse and kaolin.

Glaze : petuntse, sometimes softened by addition of lime.

Body and glaze fired at one operation, so that the glaze receives the fiercest heat given.

Glassy or fritted porcelain (St. Cloud, Vieux Sèvres, Bow, and Chelsea).

Body, or paste : largely glass or frit, with a small proportion of white clay.

Glaze : a very fusible glass made from red lead, nitre, sand, etc.

The first operation was the preparation of the glass or frit. Some of the later English frits were not very glassy, and contained bone-ash.

The body was fired to what is known as the "biscuit" condition, and the glaze was fired subsequently at a lower temperature.

English bone-porcelain (practically all English factories of the nineteenth century).

Body, or paste : bone-ash, china stone, china clay.

Glaze : china stone and china clay, with boracic acid, alkalies, and lead oxide.

The body is fired first to what is known as the "biscuit" condition, and the glaze is fired subsequently at a lower temperature.

It will be evident that from such differences of material and treatment there must be equally striking differences in the appearance and qualities of the different kinds of porcelain. The differences between true porcelain and glassy porcelain are, of course, very strongly marked, so that it should be absolutely impossible for instance, to confound a piece of early Bow or Chelsea with a Plymouth or Bristol piece.

In addition to these three principal forms of porcelain which were perfected in Europe during the eighteenth century, it must be stated that a number of other porcelains were invented in the nineteenth century which, like English bone-porcelain, combine some of the qualities of true and of artificial porcelains. The first step in this direction was taken about 1845 at the works of Messrs. Copeland & Garrett, of Stoke-on-Trent, in the introduction of the porcelain body known as Parian.* This mixture is composed of the ingredients of the body of true porcelain, but they are used in different proportions. Where, for instance, a true porcelain body would be made by mixing almost equal parts of the fusible constituent (petuntse) and the infusible constituent (kaolin), a common mixture for the Parian body would be two parts of felspar (the fusible constituent of petuntse) and one part of kaolin.† This particular form of porcelain can be fired in the biscuit stage so as to assume a dull sheen becoming at the same time practically impervious to staining fluids. Its use in this direction will be described in the detailed account of the work of modern factories. It differs from " true "

* This name was given to the substance because of the resemblance of the body, in its biscuit condition, to Parian marble.

† In some of the early types of Parian the fusibility was increased by the addition of glass, but this practice has now been generally abandoned.

FIG. 3.— INO AND BACCHUS. MODELLED
BY J. H. FOLEY, R.A.

COPELAND'S PARIAN.

porcelain in the composition of the body, and still further, when it is glazed, by the fact that a glaze of the ordinary English porcelain type is melted on it at a lower temperature than that needed to " biscuit " the ware.

On the Continent, too, the extreme hardness of the glaze of true porcelain and the consequent difficulty of obtaining certain decorative effects on it, have led to the production of intermediate forms of porcelain such as the new porcelains of Sèvres and Berlin. In the case of the new porcelain of Sèvres, for instance, the true porcelain body is rendered more siliceous and less aluminous by the addition of pure sand to the petuntse and kaolin, and the glaze is rendered more fusible by the addition of lime; thus the firing temperature required is now only about 1,350° C., instead of 1,450° C. to 1,500° C., and the glaze is so much softer that the on-glaze colours sink into it, becoming richer in quality and more like those of Vieux Sèvres. At Berlin the processes have been somewhat different, but the practical results are the same.

It is no longer possible, therefore, to speak of three kinds of porcelain only ; there is a whole series of porcelains of which one extreme is the true porcelain and the other is artificial or glassy porcelain, with almost every gradation of composition and quality between them.

The terms " hard paste " and " soft paste," which have been used for many years now as convenient labels for the different kinds of porcelain, can no longer be used, except in a special sense. It used to be said that porcelain on which a steel file or the point of a knife would make no impression was " hard paste " (meaning true porcelain), and that porcelain which could be touched by a file was " soft paste," or artificial porcelain. Such a test was never a very reliable one; it no longer serves a useful purpose, and ought to be abandoned. It is quite easy to produce porcelains with bone-ash or steatite, or mixtures like Parian, which cannot be scratched by a steel point ; yet the differences between such porcelains and the true porcelain of the Chinese are profound.

There is a sense in which the terms " hard paste " and " soft paste " are absolutely accurate, and that is the sense in which the working potter would use such phrases. To him the term " hard paste " always indicates that the mixture is an infusible one, and needs a very high temperature to bring it to perfection ; while, on the contrary, " soft paste " indicates a mixture which can be sufficiently fired at a very much lower temperature. Regarded in this way, all the known forms of porcelain arrange themselves in a regular series, in which glassy porcelain needs the lowest temperature and true porcelain the highest, with English bone porcelain about midway between them.

As a rough-and-ready indication the " fracture " of the various kinds of porcelain is really of more value than the hardness as tested by a steel point. The fracture of true porcelain is almost conchoidal (like that of a flint pebble), and the fractured surface is quite vitreous and practically impervious to staining fluids. The fracture of glassy porcelain is quite irregular ; the fractured surface is about as granular as a piece of lump sugar, and it readily absorbs staining fluids.

Glassy porcelains and bone porcelains have the defect that they are more liable to crack from sudden changes of temperature than true porcelain is ; but, on the other hand, the glaze of true porcelain is more readily " chipped," or flaked off the edges of pieces, than is the case with the glaze of English porcelain ; and it is often possible to distinguish the various kinds by this test alone.

It must be said, however, that probably the best test is in the trained eye of the connoisseur. The felspathic glaze of true porcelain is almost always full of minute bubbles, too small to be separately distinguished by the unaided eye, but producing a soft and slightly opalescent effect, to which true porcelain in a large measure owes its charm of surface. The fact, too, that the glaze of true porcelain is fired along with the body at the highest temperature, causes an intimate union to take place between them which gives a feeling of depth to the glaze. The brilliant glaze of artificial or bone porcelain always lacks this depth and quality, but it possesses a great advantage in all over-glaze decoration, as, owing to its fusibility, the enamel colours sink into the glaze and become enriched, by this incorporation with the glaze, in a way that is noticeably lacking in the enamel colours on the glaze of true porcelain. If we choose illustrations from the eighteenth century English wares, the difference between the enamel painting on the artificial porcelains of Chelsea and Bow, and that on the porcelains of Plymouth or of Bristol is most striking. In the former case the enamel colour sinks into the glaze and becomes one with it ; in the latter, the enamel colour always stands up on the glaze, and is frequently quite dull and dry in surface. As in every other form of decorative art, the methods of porcelain decoration have been influenced by the nature of the materials, and some idea of this influence may be gathered from the following pages.

CHAPTER IV.

THE FOREIGN SOURCES OF ENGLISH DESIGN:

In the previous chapters the fact has been clearly established that English porcelain was an imported and not an indigenous manufacture. In the beginning, at all events, its materials and its methods were derived from the experience gained in other countries. Such art as is displayed in connection with it was even more distinctly " foreign " in its origin, and it is necessary that some attempt should be made to summarise briefly the various sources from which the English potters and pot painters of the eighteenth century drew their ideas and inspirations. When the earliest English factories of which there is any definite record were started—in 1745-1751—there were in the market only three kinds of porcelain—the Oriental porcelain imported by the India Companies ; the true porcelain of Dresden ; and the artificial porcelain of France. All these kinds of porcelain were vastly admired by the collectors and connoisseurs of the day, and as the Englishman was then, as now, more workman than artist, his first tendency, naturally, was to copy the pieces so greatly admired and so highly prized, as faithfully as his fingers and his wit would allow him.

It must also be remembered that at this time our native English pottery was only taking its first steps from primitive simplicity, and that, too, in a part of the country remote from the capital, so that at Bow, Chelsea, and Worcester there was no body of trained workmen or painters with hereditary or acquired skill, but everything had to be built up " from the ground." Take the early advertisement put out from the Bow factory in 1753 :—

Painters brought up in the snuff-box way, japanning, fan-painting, etc., may have opportunities of trial ; wherein if they succeed, they shall have due encouragement.

N.B.—At the same house, a person is wanted who can model small figures in clay neatly.*

And also the " Case of the Undertaker of the Chelsea Manufacture of Porcelain Ware," where it is stated that the Chelsea works has " a nursery of thirty lads taken from the parishes and charity schools and bred to designing and painting—arts very much wanted here." No further proof can be needed that the proprietors and directors of these early factories were absolute pioneers, and if their pieces sometimes appear to us as childish, even ludicrous, attempts to reproduce the styles of other porcelains, the fault is probably due quite as much to the want of a sound taste in the public for whom they were intended as to the inexperience of the potters themselves.

In many cases the influence of foreign productions was openly acknowledged, as, for instance, when the works at Bow were described as "New Canton," or those at Worcester as the " Newly-established Tonquin Factory." In the same way, at the first sale of Derby porcelain in London, the pieces were advertised as "After the finest Dresden models," † while in the catalogue of the 1784 sale of Duesbury's Derby and Chelsea porcelain, it is stated that the objects are " of the most delicate approved patterns and shapes, finished in a style of superior richness and elegance from the choicest specimens of the Seve, Dresden, Berlin, and Monsieur manufactures." A better instance of the tradesman seeking to flatter the supposed taste of his public would be difficult to find. After this it is easy to understand, though impossible to excuse, the use of forged marks—or, at all events, marks calculated to deceive —on the productions of many English factories. It would be easier to say offhand which of the English factories of the eighteenth century used marks that might easily be mistaken for the crossed

* This advertisement appeared in *Aris's Birmingham Gazette,* November 5th, 1753.

† *Public Advertiser,* December, 1756. *See* Nightingale, folio lxvii.

swords of Dresden or the double " L's " of Vincennes and Sèvres, than which did not.

This foreign influence which was so strongly marked in the artistic development of English porcelain will, of course, be discussed in detail in the subsequent accounts of the separate factories, but it will be convenient here to take a general view of those decorative ideas and motives which were commonly used throughout the industry. Oriental porcelain was most highly prized, and the earliest decorative ideas seem to have been drawn from that source. Every collector is familiar with the beautiful white Chinese pieces, where the qualities of the paste and glaze are shown at their very best. Among the productions of Bow and Chelsea will be found many pieces of white ware, in which the early glassy porcelain of those factories is made to reveal its quality in the same way. In Fig. 4 will be found reproductions of a Bow piece and two Chelsea pieces of this simple white ware with embossed ornament as its sole decoration, and, for comparison, an actual Chinese piece. The Bow piece is decorated with a sprig of the well-known " Prunus " pattern, separately moulded and stuck on, so that the detail as well as the method of decoration is due to Chinese influence ; but the modelled ornament on the Chelsea pieces is not at all Chinese in character. An illustration of a Worcester sugar-bowl is given in Fig. 45, where the Chinese device of relieving white on white has been carried out in a very simple English way, but with absolutely delightful results. Oriental blue and white pieces also came in for a great share of attention and imitation. In some cases every effort was made to copy Oriental designs and to obtain the closest possible approximation to the original both in drawing and in colour. The English bodies and glazes were so different from the Chinese, however, that even had the touch of the painters been comparable, the final result would have been strikingly different. The most successful results were obtained at Worcester in the early period of the soapstone body, when the quality of the blue and white produced was remarkably good. On Plate II. will be found three

FIG. 4.—RAISED ORNAMENT - WHITE, ON WHITE
GROUND. A, CHELSEA CUP. B, CHELSEA
GOAT AND BEE CREAM JUG. C, BOW
CUP. D, CHINESE BOWL.

pieces of English blue and white : a Bow mug, a Chelsea plate, and a Worcester mug ; from which it is quite possible to judge the qualities of blue and white obtained at those places. It has often been asserted that the painters at some of the English factories became so expert in copying Chinese figures and designs that their work is almost indistinguishable from Chinese painting. It is difficult to imagine how such an idea can have arisen, for the differences in the "touch," as well as in the method of Oriental and European painters, are most strongly marked. Apart altogether from variations due to the difference between " true " and " artificial " porcelain materials and methods, the way in which Chinese blue is floated on to the piece, and the nervous, yet precise, touch of the outlines are generally in the very greatest contrast to the technique of the English pot-painter. An attempt has been made to illustrate these differences by photographing together bits of detail from two very good pieces of English painted blue and white and two ordinary Chinese pieces, on as large a scale as possible (Figs. 5–8). The Bow dragon is well painted, but not nearly so well as the Chinese dragon, while the bit of Worcester foliage is greatly inferior in technique to the Chinese piece, although that is by no means an extraordinarily good example.

The Oriental pieces in many-coloured decoration also furnished our pot-painters with many telling designs. The well-known designs of Kakiyemon—a skilled potter of Imari, in the province of Hizen, who flourished in the latter half of the seventeenth century*— seem to have had a particular fascination for the painters of Bow ; and the famous " partridge," or " quail and wheatsheaf " pattern of that factory is copied almost exactly from these Japanese pieces. Many forms of it occur—indeed, a whole series of " Kakiyemon " designs were produced at Bow, Chelsea, Worcester, Bristol, and elsewhere. A prettier style cf decoration could hardly be imagined, considering the materials and resources of our early potters, and many of the pieces of this class, with their bright touches of red

---

* Bushell says that Kakiyemon introduced at Imari the art of decorating porcelain by means of vitrifiable colours relieved with gold as early as 1647.

and gold on a creamy ground, are charming examples of the work
of their respective factories. Plate IV. reproduces three pieces
of this class—a Bow, a Chelsea, and a Worcester plate—as well
as a Japanese piece of the kind from which the designs were
obviously adapted.

Among later English designs inspired by the later and more
ordinary kinds of Imari porcelain special mention should be made
of the Crown-Derby Japan patterns (*see* Plate XII.). In this case
the patterns produced were hardly copies of any definite pattern
so much as mixed designs from various sources, and it must be
said that their bold scheme of colour is often very fine, and in
some cases actually superior to Japanese pieces of the same class.
The red is not too red ; in the thin touches it is distinctly orange,
and harmonises better with the blue and gold than the red of
the Japanese pieces.

In some of the patterns of the Kakiyemon style we often find
the little partridges or quails of the earlier pieces replaced by more
ornate birds, reminiscent of the gorgeous pheasants and birds of
paradise of the East. Gradually the birds became more and more
wonderful, until we reach the class of pieces decorated with exotic
bird designs, in which the creatures are seen to be purely the products of imagination, designed to exhibit the pot-painter's skill
and the resources of his palette. These later birds were probably
copied from Chinese rice-paper drawings, or from the gorgeous,
painted wall-papers and embroideries that at this period were
being imported by the noble and the wealthy for the decoration
of their mansions.*

These elaborated " birds " seem to have been first used in
England † on Chelsea pieces, but Worcester, Bristol, and many
later factories have also used them largely ; indeed, they became
almost the chief feature in the designs of one period of the

* In Chippendale's well-known work, the " Gentleman and Cabinet Maker's
Director," London, 1762, illustrations are found of chair covers, etc., ornamented
with the same curious birds.

† Kakiyemon designs and exotic birds were largely copied at Dresden and
other Continental factories, as well as in England.

PLATE IV.

Kakiyemon Designs.

Victoria and Albert Museum.

(*See pp.* 27-28.)

JAPANESE.   WORCESTER.

CHELSEA.   BOW.

Worcester factory. The illustration given in Figs. 9 and 10 shows
a Chelsea dish and a Worcester dish with this decoration. and is
of special interest because it proves that the shape of the Chelsea
dish as well as the design had been copied at the latter factory. We
know that some of the Chelsea painters migrated to Worcester
after 1764, and this migration probably accounts for these pieces
and many others which will be mentioned in the account of the
Worcester factory. In the later pieces the birds are generally
painted in white panels, surrounded by scale-blue ground and
rich gilding, as in the example on Plate XV. The decoration
of the Coalport cup in Fig. 68 serves to show how persistently
this motive was used on English porcelain.

If Oriental pieces gave the first impetus to our porcelain
painters, the influence of the European potteries was soon also
felt by them, and ultimately became paramount. The advertisement quoted on page 25 shows how Duesbury, of Derby, a shrewd
business man, appealed to his patrons in 1784, and there is no
doubt that from 1750 onwards the English potters studied most
carefully the shapes and decorations of both French and German
porcelain, and frequently tried hard to reproduce them. Often,
of course, these shapes and designs " were repeated with a difference." and while there can be no doubt as to the original source
from which a design or a style was derived, there is sufficient
variety in the treatment or execution to preserve it from the charge
of mere plagiarism. It must not be forgotten that many of the
Continental porcelain factories were largely subsidised by their
kings and princes, so that it was possible for them to secure the
services of distinguished artists as designers of shapes and decorations. The English factories had no such support, but had to
depend for their success on meeting the taste of the public; and in
copying Dresden figures, raised " flowering," and delicate lace-work,
Chantilly sprigs, Sèvres roses, festoons of laurel, intertwining
ribbon borders, and elaborately painted figure groups, they evidently gave their patrons complete satisfaction. It has become
the fashion now to affect an air of superiority in speaking of these

earlier forms of pottery decoration, but considering all the factors that determine what shall be done in painting " on glaze," it would be difficult to find a more appropriate style than that of these early patterns for the decoration of china tea and coffee cups, and all the etceteras of the table. It says something for the Englishmen, at all events, that the patterns they selected were often the best available, and in all artistic matters the question of selection is an important part of the problem.

Mention must also be made of the sources whence the statuettes and groups produced in such profusion at Bow, Chelsea, and Derby were derived. Some of them were undoubtedly modelled by sculptors of eminence, for we know that Bacon produced models for Bow and possibly for Chelsea and Derby, and Roubiliac produced many important figures and groups for Chelsea. The names of other sculptors and modellers of lesser repute, such as Rossi, Stephan, and Spengler, who modelled at Derby, are also known. Many figures are direct imitations or reproductions of Dresden and Sèvres models, and we have quite a large number of figures modelled from contemporary drawings and engravings. Some of these latter figures are of remarkable elegance, and it says much for their unknown modellers that the translation from the flat to the round was managed with such skill and sympathy. The frontispiece is a notable illustration of this. If, as we have reason to suppose, this figure was copied from the figure of " a lady dancing a minuet," in the well-known engraving of Watteau's " Fêtes Venitiennes,"* it is delightful to see how far the grace and charm of the great French artist have been preserved. The companion male figure will also be found in the Schreiber Collection (Victoria and Albert Museum), but in this case the rendering is not quite so perfect, and the actual specimen in question seems to have suffered a little in the hands of the potter when he was " sticking up " the separately moulded parts. How expressive these figures are of the spirit of their age is shown, too, by the

* The engraving in question can be found on a screen in the Ceramic Gallery, Victoria and Albert Museum.

FIG. 5.—PAINTING IN UNDER-GLAZE BLUE.
CHINESE.

FIG. 6.—PAINTING IN UNDER-GLAZE BLUE.
CHINESE.

FIG. 7.—PAINTING IN UNDER-GLAZE BLUE.
WORCESTER.

FIG. 8.—PAINTING IN UNDER-GLAZE BLUE.
BOW.

decoration which the enameller or pot-painter has added to them. In the figure reproduced the little sprays of flowers with which the lady's dress is sown form an ornamental treatment absolutely in keeping with the spirit of the figure itself, a fresh and almost unexpected illustration of the fact that in the middle of the eighteenth century a real feeling for art was alive even in those who followed so humble a vocation as the enamelling of china figures.

In the first half of the period (1750–1800) all the varied influences so rapidly reviewed were at work, generally speaking, with successful results ; but from 1780 to 1800 the utmost confusion of styles set in, and Chinese, Japanese, French, and German shapes and designs were thrown together into a most incongruous mixture. Unfortunately, too, the revival of interest in Greek vases which followed the publication of Sir William Hamilton's " Antiquités Etrusques " in 1766–67, and the commercial success of Wedgwood's reproductions of classic shapes in his fine dry bodies, added to the confusion. " Classic shapes," as they were called, became a rage among the porcelain makers, in spite of the fact that they were not well adapted for reproduction in porcelain, and that many of them were originally metal, and not pottery shapes at all. To complete the tale of disaster, the working conditions of the factories changed too—Bow, Chelsea, and Bristol were abandoned ; Dr. Wall, of Worcester, died in 1776 ; the Derby firm became still more commercial in spirit ; and in place of a number of small factories, at each of which a little group of workmen carried out the ideas of a man who was an enthusiast, the trade was practically absorbed by a few large factories, which belonged to, and were managed by, men who were, for the most part, " commercial " by instinct and by training. No doubt this organisation led to more technically perfect production on the whole, but its immediate results were disastrous from the point of view of art and taste. For more than sixty years English porcelain remained under a cloud so far as any real artistic spirit was concerned, and it was left for the great modern factories to show that it was possible to produce, under the altered conditions, pieces worthy to rank with the best artificial porcelains of the eighteenth century.

Some illustrations of the pieces produced in this period (1780–1850), with their uninteresting forms, painfully even ground colours, tasteless painted or printed patterns, and over-elaborate gilding, will be found in the accounts of the separate factories. The late eighteenth century Worcester plates on Plate XVII., the Derby plates on Plate XI., the Spode vases in Fig. 77, and the Coalport dessert plate made for royalty in 1850 and shown in Fig. 69 are perfect examples of this phase of the potter's art. It must in fairness be said that the Continental factories suffered a very similar eclipse during the same period, so that it is not surprising that the earlier English porcelains have received such enthusiastic commendation from connoisseurs, and are so highly prized by collectors.

Fig. 9.—DISH WITH EXOTIC BIRDS.
CHELSEA.

Fig. 10.—DISH WITH EXOTIC BIRDS.
WORCESTER.

CHAPTER V.

CHELSEA.

IN any detailed account of the English porcelain factories and their productions the post of honour must be awarded to Chelsea, not merely because the earliest dated specimens of English porcelain are the small white cream jugs of the goat and bee pattern (*see* Fig. 4 B), which had "Chelsea, 1745," scratched into the paste before firing, but also because the figures, vases, and other articles of the Chelsea factory were, during the first twenty years or so of its existence—1750-1770—the finest and most ambitious pieces produced in England, rivalling indeed the productions of the royal factory of Sèvres. Of the actual foundation of the factory we have no exact knowledge. The two pieces already mentioned, and certain similar pieces, such as the well-known crawfish salt-cellars, of which there are good specimens in the British Museum, and which may fairly be referred to the earliest period of this factory, show that whoever may have been their producer had a first-rate body and glaze of glassy porcelain at his command. Whether this indicates that the factory had already been in existence for a number of years, as some writers assert, or, as has been suggested in an earlier chapter of this book,* that these pieces are the production of some French workmen from St. Cloud or Chantilly, there is no further mention of the factory until the year 1747, when R. Campbell (who seems to have been well acquainted with the various handicrafts carried on in London), writes in his *London Tradesman :*

"We have lately made some attempts to make porcelain or china ware after the manner it is done in China and Dresden ; there is a house at

* *See* page 9.

D

Greenwich and another at Chelsea, where the undertakers have been for some time trying to imitate that beautiful manufacture."

There is also Shaw's statement * : " That a number of Staffordshire potters (including a slip-maker, a thrower, a turner, a fireman, and a painter) left Burslem in 1747, to work at the Chelsea China Manufactory. They soon ascertained that they were the principal workmen, on whose exertion all the excellence of the porcelain must depend ; they then resolved to commence business on their own account at Chelsea, and were in some degree successful ; but at length they abandoned it and returned to Burslem."

It must be said that Shaw is no very reliable authority, and, but that there is a fair amount of evidence that his date was correct, the statement would be unworthy of notice here. The belief of the Staffordshire potters that they were the men on whose exertions the success of the factory was to depend, must be dismissed with a smile ; they could have had absolutely no knowledge of porcelain making, or of the composition of body and glaze suitable for such a purpose ; the Chelsea factory evidently existed before they left Staffordshire, and their departure made no difference to its success. If they did set up an establishment for making porcelain in Chelsea, it was probably at the expense of some enthusiast, and they, no doubt, returned to Staffordshire when his patience or his purse became exhausted.

It is believed that a Mr. Charles Gouyn was the manager of the factory at this date (1747), and it has been stated by various writers that the Duke of Cumberland and Sir Everard Fawkner, his secretary and Postmaster-General, were the real proprietors, but it is difficult to find any solid grounds for the statement. There would be nothing inherently improbable in the supposition that the Chelsea factory was established or actively supported by royalty, for it was almost a fashion at this period, with the sovereign princes of the Continent, to subsidise a porcelain factory. The early kings and princes of the Hanoverian line in England were not, however, noted either for their patronage of the arts or their liberality, and

---

* Shaw's " History of the Staffordshire Potteries," Hanley, 1828 ; p. 167.

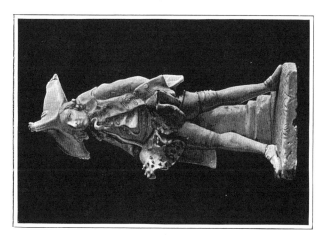

FIG. 13.—WOODWARD AS "THE FINE GENTLEMAN." STATUETTE IN WHITE CHELSEA.

FIG. 12.—SEATED LADY. STATUETTE IN WHITE. **CHELSEA.**

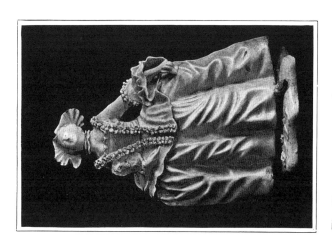

FIG. 11.—KITTY CLIVE AS "MRS. RIOT." STATUETTE IN WHITE. **CHELSEA.**

the only patronage that can safely be ascribed to the English royalty or nobility of the period, amounts to nothing more than an occasional commission for an expensive service or the provision of some piece of Oriental material or French or German porcelain to furnish a design or a model for English imitation. While there is no direct evidence that the Duke of Cumberland had pecuniary interests in the venture, there is evidence which seems conclusive on the other side. In the *General Advertiser* of January 17th, 1750, an advertisement appeared, mentioning " Mr. Charles Gouyn, late proprietor and chief manager of the Chelsea House "; and in the same advertisement M. Sprimont is described as the manager of the Chelsea factory.* Bearing on the same point is the evidence of the well-known " Case of the Undertaker of the Chelsea Manufacture of Porcelain Ware,"† which seems to have been published after 1752, as it mentions the " late Duke of Orleans," who died in that year. Reference is made in this document to the patronage of Continental factories by their kings, queens, and princes, but no mention of any similar patronage at Chelsea. The whole document is, indeed, a plea against the contraband trade in Dresden porcelain,‡ that appears to have been openly managed from the house of the Saxon minister. We may be perfectly certain that if the Duke of Cumberland or King George II., as has been elsewhere asserted, had possessed a pecuniary interest in the factory, there would have been no need to put forward the " Case of the Undertaker of the Chelsea Manufactory," begging that the Custom House Officers should do their duty and enforce the law.

This advertisement of 1750 is the first mention of Sprimont that we have in connection with Chelsea, but there is plenty of later information concerning him, for he remained the manager,

* *See* J. E. Nightingale's " Contributions toward the History of English Porcelain," fol. v.

† Lansdowne MSS., British Museum, vol. 829, fol. 21 ; also quoted at length by Jewitt.

‡ Jonas Hanway, writing in 1750-51, says : " It is a subject of horror to see so many shops supplied with the porcelain of Dresden, though it is importable only under oath of being for private use, and not for sale."

undertaker, or proprietor of the Chelsea factory throughout the
period of its greatest excellence and down to its sale to
W. Duesbury, of Derby, in 1770. It was under the management
or proprietorship of Sprimont that most of the Chelsea porcelain
remaining to us was produced, and it is to his taste and influence
that we must ascribe the early success of the factory. He seems
to have been originally a silversmith of Compton Street, Soho, and
his name was entered as a plate-worker at Goldsmiths' Hall in
January, 1742.* His training in metal-work obviously influenced
the manner and style of the earlier productions of Chelsea. It
has also been suggested that Sprimont's training accounts for the
production of the florid and rococo pieces of later days. Against
this view it should be noted that he was most closely and
actively concerned in the management of the factory during the
earlier period of its existence. After 1756–1757 he was frequently
ailing and very lame, so that presumably his influence could
hardly have been so constant and direct after that time. It
does seem, however, that his natural bent led him toward the
production of sumptuous and elegant ornamental pieces for the
decoration of the table, the sideboard, the toilet, or the china-
closet, rather than to the safer but less brilliant policy of making
plates, cups, saucers, dishes, and the thousand and one things
of common use. It has been proved over and over again in England that a pottery works (at least, of any importance) cannot be
established and carried on with success merely for the production
of what may be called cabinet pieces. Several eighteenth century
china factories (and among them that of Chelsea) might have had
a longer lease of life had this fact been recognised by their
managers ; but the business of this chapter is not with what
might have been done at Chelsea, but with what was done.

As to the exact site of the factory, or factories, where Chelsea
china was produced, there has long been an idea that they were
situated close to Chelsea Old Church, and in the neighbourhood of
Lawrence Street. In 1843, during the excavation of foundations

* Church's " English Porcelain," p. 16.

for some new houses in Cheyne Row West, large quantities of broken vases and figures were found, showing that the factory must have been in that vicinity, but more definite information was lacking. Recently, however, Mr. Bemrose has published copies of old leases in his possession * which make it clear that the site of the Chelsea factory in the later period of its existence was at the corner of Lawrence Street and Justice Walk, as stated in Faulkner's " History of Chelsea." These documents, which are of the greatest interest, show that Sprimont in 1759 leased for the term of fourteen years two adjacent plots of land. One portion had formerly been in the possession of a Mr. Largrave, and by him apparently sub-let to Sprimont, but the other portion had been in the direct tenure of Sprimont himself, who had previously erected on it " several workhouses, shops, and kilns for the manufacturing of porcelain." A careful consideration of the documents seems to show that at this period (1759) Sprimont was desirous of extending the factory and workshops he had built, and while securing a fresh lease of the ground he already held, he also secured the direct lease of an adjoining piece belonging to the same owner but previously rented from Mr. Largrave, who presumably had no connection with the porcelain business. This view receives confirmation from what we know as to the doings of the factory. Operations slackened in 1757, and had almost ceased in the early part of 1758, owing to the illness of Sprimont, but they were resumed in 1758–1759 with renewed vigour, and the fine pieces with richly coloured grounds, for which Chelsea is famous above all other English factories, date from this period. At this time, if ever, there would be such an accession of business as to render an extension of the premises desirable.

The productions of the factory during the period when Sprimont was its proprietor were most varied in style and quality. Down to about 1754–1756 the great proportion of objects produced seem to have been sparingly, even reticently, decorated. The natural

* " Bow, Chelsea, and Derby Porcelain," by William Bemrose, p. 20 *et seq.*

beauty of the material was allowed to display itself, with the most satisfactory results. Indeed, it would be impossible to wish for anything more perfect in texture and tone than the rich fritted body of early Chelsea production. Its resemblance in appearance to the glassy porcelains of St. Cloud and Chantilly has often been commented upon.* The body and the glaze were exceedingly soft and fusible, so that the pieces preserved in collections frequently show signs of warping and distortion in the firing. It is impossible even to suggest what proportion of the pieces was absolutely unsaleable, but it must have been very large.

It cannot be said that this early ware is remarkable for the excellence of its " potting " ; the pieces are often, indeed, so thick as to be quite opaque. In the thin parts, particularly in the sides of deep plates and dishes, the ware is, however, beautifully transparent, and frequently exhibits a feature to which attention was first drawn by Dr. W. H. Diamond. He observed that many early Chelsea pieces, when carefully scrutinised in a strong light, or by viewing a candle through them in a dark room, showed a number of little round discs more transparent than the rest of the mass, and somewhat irregularly scattered through it. It has been suggested that these are due to irregular and excessive aggregation of the vitreous frit which formed such a large proportion of the paste. This is undoubtedly true, but the reason for their existence is that the Chelsea body was extremely liable to go out of shape, and, in endeavouring to correct this fault, the Chelsea potters hit on the plan of keeping some of the frit fairly coarse, instead of grinding it all to an impalpable powder—a most workmanlike method of dealing with such a difficult problem as the firing of a glassy porcelain.

The decorations of these first period pieces consist almost exclusively of sprays of flowers and leaves, exotic plants, insects, and butterflies, irregularly scattered about the pieces, with portions of the modelled ornament, particularly the edges of

* *See* Sir A. W. Franks, " Notes on Chelsea Porcelain," *Archæological Journal,* 1862.

PLATE V.

Chelsea Trinkets, Seals, Étuis, and Scent Bottles.

Franks Collection : British Museum.

(*See pp.* 41-42.)

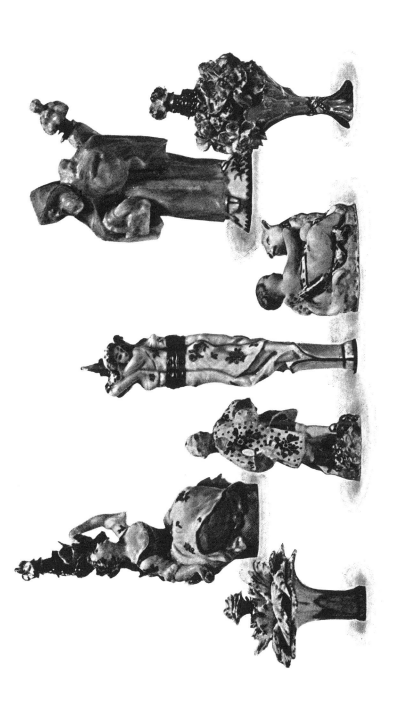

dishes and cups and the scroll-work bases of the figures, very simply lined in colours, and, occasionally, in gold. The general appearance of the early pieces often suggests the influence of Dresden and of Oriental models ; while the decoration is such as could naturally be expected of those not specially skilled in pottery painting, but brought up rather in " the enamelling, japanning, and fan-painting way," as the earliest painters must have been.

It can never be said with absolute certainty that these early pieces, even when they bear the Chelsea mark, were decorated at the Chelsea works.* From a very early period in the history of china-making in England we know that a number of painters made a practice of buying white pieces and decorating them, either for the London dealers or for private persons. Mr. Bemrose has published, in the work already alluded to,† facsimiles of some pages of the work-book of William Duesbury (afterwards the proprietor of the Derby factory), dated 1751–53, in which he enters particulars of work done in this way for various London dealers. The pieces enamelled were mostly figures, but some few jars, flowers, " branches " (candlesticks ?), and other articles are mentioned. In many cases their origin is stated as Chelsea, Bow, Derby, and Staffordshire, and from the number of articles enamelled within a given time, there is no doubt that Duesbury not only enamelled himself, but had a regular workshop, and employed a number of enamellers to work for him. We have plenty of evidence that quantities of white pieces (*i.e.* glazed and not decorated) were sold from both Chelsea and Bow, so that there would be no difficulty in colouring or decorating the pieces to the requirements of the dealers. This was all the easier, as the favourite method of decoration in vogue was that of " enamelling," or painting in enamel colours, on the surface of the fired white glaze. The piece was then re-fired in a small muffle kiln, at a temperature which, while insufficient to re-melt the glaze, fused

---

* This statement is equally applicable to early pieces of Bow, Derby, and Worcester.

† " Bow, Chelsea, and Derby Porcelain," pp. 8, etc.

the enamel colour firmly into it. All the red, brown, yellow, and green colours, as well as the gold, used on early porcelain were fired in this way on the surface of the fired glaze ; very much as if they had been painted on glass, in fact. Blue was the only colour used under the glaze, and the slight use of blue on the early ornamental productions of the factory is quite noticeable.

Every collector of early English porcelains owes a debt of gratitude to the late Mr. J. E. Nightingale for the care and assiduity with which he ran to earth contemporary press notices, advertisements, and catalogues of the periodical sales of the early English factories.* With the information thus procured, many disputed points have been decided, and on studying these notices of Chelsea productions, in conjunction with the actual pieces that are preserved in various collections, a very sharp division between the earlier and later productions of the factory can be established.

The pieces which may with safety be attributed to the early period—*i.e.* earlier than 1756—group themselves into several well-marked classes :—

1. *White pieces.*—The goat and bee cream-jug, the crawfish salts, shell, and rockwork salts, small sauce-boats and cups without handles, such as the examples in Fig. 4 A and B.

2. *Pieces with decorations after the Oriental manner.*—Square and hexagonal cups, saucers, plates, and dishes, generally decorated in the Japanese style. Much useful ware of this class was produced throughout the existence of the factory. It is often decorated in blue under-glaze, in imitation of the Chinese pieces (*see* Plate II.), or in red and gold on the glaze after the designs of Kakiyemon and other potters of the province of Hizen, in Japan. (*See* Plate IV.)

3. *Leaf dishes of various shapes and sizes.*—The early pieces are

* J. E. Nightingale, " Contributions toward the History of Early English Porcelain." 1881.

generally decorated with a brown or pink lined edge, and have the veins of the leaves touched in with the same colour. When the edges of such pieces are gilded the piece is almost certainly of later make. In later pieces, too, the edges of each leaf were often washed in with bands of a strong florid green and a somewhat opaque yellow green, producing a decidedly vulgar effect. On the early pieces, in addition to the veining, little sprays of flowers, leaves, insects (particularly ladybirds) were often irregularly scattered over the pieces, and used, as potters always use such bits of independent ornament, to hide slight defects or flaws, which would have made the piece unsaleable as a white piece.

4. *Vessels for table use or ornament in fantastic shapes.*—Tureens, dishes, sauce-boats, plates, and pickle trays were largely produced, modelled and coloured in the most naturalistic manner to represent animals, fruit, vegetables, birds, and fish. Cabbages, cauliflowers, bundles of asparagus, apples, lemons, oranges, and melons may be mentioned as forming one such group. A boar's head, ducks, a hen and chickens on large oval stand with sunflowers and foliage in relief, a dish and cover formed as a group of two doves, rabbits, swans, and carp go to form another.

It is interesting to note in passing that at this very period Whieldon and Josiah Wedgwood, then in partnership in Staffordshire, were also producing in their earthenware, cauliflower, melon, and pineapple pieces.

5. *Handles for knives and forks.*—These were produced in great variety, and are frequently mentioned in the sale lists of the period with great commendation.

6. *Porcelain trinkets and toys.*—The famous Chelsea trinkets, small and delicately modelled figures, bouquets, animals, groups, and single heads, intended to be mounted

in gold (sometimes even set with jewels) and to be worn on chains as scent bottles, *étuis*, seals, or toys, certainly made their appearance in this first period. There can be no doubt, however, that the trade in these little articles of luxury proved a remunerative one, and that their production continued down to the close of the factory. Plate V. shows a group of these charming pieces from the Franks collection at the British Museum, but it is evident from the lavish use of gold and colour that many of the actual specimens shown were made in the period between 1759 and 1768.

7. *Statuettes and groups of figures.*—From a very early period Chelsea was famous for the production of statuettes, and as the activity in this direction continued to the end, it is hardly too much to say that the Chelsea figures surpassed in number and importance all those of the other contemporary English factories combined. The difficulties of dating any given figure-piece accurately are undoubtedly great, but it is probable that the smaller and simpler figures and groups, slightly decorated and with very little gold, were produced first. The taste and skill shown in the modelling of some of these early figures have been commended in the last chapter. Among these early figures mention may be made of the bust of the Duke of Cumberland, figures emblematical of the Continents, the Seasons, and the Senses, and the monkey orchestra, probably in imitation of Dresden. Along with these early figures must be classed the birds perched on stumps, and enamelled in naturalistic colours, of which there is such a wonderful collection in the Schreiber bequest. Artistically these bird figures are of no account, but they were evidently produced in quantity, and as many of them bear a very early mark, there can be little doubt as to their period.

8. *Green Camaieu decoration.* It is probable that the pieces of this class were produced during the early years, but the decoration may have been continued in the later period too. Dishes, plates, and particularly trinket sets composed of a number of small pieces fitting together to form a tray for the toilet table, were frequently decorated in this way. On a perfectly white ground, landscapes, often with ruins, were finely outlined in purple and then a very glossy green enamel was thickly washed over the scene. The process is singularly like that used in the Chinese "Famille Verte" pieces, and the idea was probably derived from that source.

Among the illustrations of Chelsea pieces in this volume we give a number of typical early pieces—namely, the goat and bee cream-jug (Fig. 4B) ; also, on the same plate, a simple fluted cup, with embossed flowers, in which the influence of Chinese methods is very strongly marked. The Chelsea plate decorated in underglaze blue, shown on Plate II., and the Chelsea dish with the Kakiyemon design, on Plate IV., prove that the Oriental influence was at all events felt in the designs and decoration of the earlier period, though perhaps never to the same extent as at Bow and Worcester. Considering that during this very period, the practice of printing designs from engraved copper-plates was being developed just across the river at York House, Battersea,* it is remarkable that we find so few traces of its use on Chelsea porcelain. It was used so sparingly as to suggest the idea that Sprimont rather shunned the process, as tending to diminish the artistic excellence of his wares.

The small white figure (Fig. 12) is a most charming example of Chelsea modelling, not only for the quality of its paste and glaze, but also for the skill and feeling with which the figure is rendered. The resemblance in treatment between this small figure and the Bow figure of a cook (*see* Fig. 27), which is

---

* Sir S. T. Jannsen's Battersea Enamel Works.

attributed with some probability to the youthful John Bacon * (afterwards famous as a sculptor), lends colour to the statement frequently made that Bacon modelled for Chelsea as well as for Bow.

The first departure from the simplicity of the early style is marked by the appearance of a few vases decorated with a rich Mazarine blue (or, as it would be now called, " gros-bleu ") ground. In the sale catalogue of 1756, a copy of which is in the British Museum, a few pieces are mentioned as being decorated with this rich blue ground. On Plate VI. will be found a reproduction of a Chelsea vase of this kind, and though this particular specimen is undoubtedly of later date (probably after 1760), it serves to illustrate perfectly the quality of the first of those rich-coloured grounds for which Chelsea afterwards became famous. The blue colour is not only of beautiful tone, being blue and not black in the deepest parts, and of a fine sapphire tint in the lighter parts, but as it was obtained by painting the mineral pigment on the biscuit ware and then covering it with glaze, the colour is always agreeably broken and uneven, and possesses in consequence a quality which the more technically perfect Mazarine blue grounds of later factories sadly lack.

During the year 1757 the production of Chelsea porcelain undoubtedly slackened, and, indeed, advertisements appeared in the *Public Advertiser* of that year (both in February and in April) saying that the operations of the factory had been much retarded by Mr. Sprimont's illness.†

Some time in 1758 the factory must have resumed operations with renewed vigour, as an important sale of its productions took place between March 19th and April 12th, 1759, and we have already seen that Sprimont took a fresh lease of his premises in the latter year.‡ It is difficult to avoid the conclusion that about this date,

---

* John Bacon, born 1740, was apprenticed to Crispe, a modeller, of Bow in 1754. He won a Society of Arts prize, for a small figure of " Peace " in 1758. He was elected A.R.A. in 1770, and R.A. in 1778. He died in 1799.

† " Nightingale," fol. xv.

‡ *See p. 37.*

which marks the commencement of the second Chelsea period, some radical change took place in the direction or management of the factory. A fresh spirit appears in every department of the work, a period of renewed experiment and development commences, and the most striking, though not the most beautiful, results in the whole history of the factory were attained. The rich, creamy appearance of the pieces of the first period has been already noticed. Though the quality of the early paste and glaze exhibits continual variations—as, indeed, was inevitable in the early days of the factory—after this date the general appearance of the white ware deteriorated, and it seems probable that a body that was rather more certain in use was produced.

Professor Church makes the very decided statement that 90 per cent. of the existing pieces of Chelsea are not of the frit body, but of the later body, which he also refers to as a bone-body. That the later body of Chelsea is very different in composition from the early body there can be no doubt. Every effort was made to discover a body mixture that would be more manageable, and therefore less costly in practice. The elaborate vases of the late period are in themselves sufficient proof that such a body had been arrived at. Bone-ash was undoubtedly used at Chelsea, for in addition to Professor Church's analyses of late Chelsea pieces, it has been found in the notes referring to the transfer of the Chelsea works to Duesbury, of Derby, that one of his first acts on obtaining possession of the works was to send ten bags of bone ash to Derby.* It is difficult, however, to believe that the Chelsea body, or, indeed, the body of any of the early factories, was a definitely settled composition. In the infancy of such an art, when knowledge was much more empirical than it is to-day, experimental bodies must have been continually produced. It is impossible to explain in any other way the great variations in the quality of pieces whose attribution to Chelsea is beyond dispute.

This change in the quality of the body is practically coincident with an equally great change in the style of decoration. Rich

* Bemrose, " Bow, Chelsea, and Derby Porcelain," p. 112.

ground colours make their appearance, and are frequently used to cover the main body of the vases, jars, cups, or dishes, reserved panels being left white to receive elaborate and careful paintings of flowers, figure compositions, and the like. (*See* Plates VI. and VIII.) Of these ground colours the pea-green is first mentioned in 1759, though it may have been obtained in the previous year; while the claret, unique among porcelain colours, was produced, along with turquoise, in 1759-60. It must be mentioned that these later Chelsea grounds—pea-green, claret or pompadour, and turquoise —differ from the Mazarine blue already described in that they are enamels—*i.e.* they are applied over the fired glaze. Owing to this fact it was much easier to produce pieces of one solid and uniform tint. With the rich, fusible glaze in use at Chelsea, these ground colours, when well fired, actually sank into the glaze so as to become perfectly incorporated with it, with the greatest gain to their brilliance and beauty. The discovery of these rich ground colours led to a revolution in the style of decoration. In place of simply-shaped pieces decorated with little sprays of flowers, insects, or birds, disposed with seeming carelessness over their surface, we have in the second period vases, jars, candelabra, ewers, and dishes, brackets, groups of figures, baskets, urns, beakers, table and tea services, as well as the little trinket pieces already noticed, richly decorated with brilliant colours, ambitious paintings, and lavish gilding.

In the notice of the sale of 1760, reference is made to " the gold peculiar to that fine and distinguished manufactory," and this self-praise was not undeserved. The gilding on the Chelsea porcelain of the second period was far superior to any gilding done on other contemporary English porcelains. The early gilding at Bow, at Longton Hall, and at Derby, was often unfired, being probably put on with " japanner's " size and merely stoved. At a later period the Bow gilding and the early Chelsea gilding were applied in the Chinese manner. Leaf gold was ground up in honey and then applied in this state to the ware, and fired until it sank into the glaze. Gilding done in this way has a somewhat dull look, and cannot be brightened by burnishing. The rich Chelsea gold was undoubtedly applied in the modern way ; an amalgam of gold and mercury was first made, and this was then ground finely with a small amount of a fusible glass or flux. In this way the gold could be worked on as thickly as necessary, and at a fairly easy fire the flux melted, securely fastening the gold to the glaze ; the gold could then be burnished and chased so as to display its utmost brilliance. Technically, this late Chelsea gilding leaves nothing to be desired, but artistically it is garish, and it was so lavishly used that the final effect is often that of mere vulgar glitter.

This growing extravagance of colour and gilding was also accompanied by a corresponding change in the forms of the pieces. Large and elaborate vases, in the most pronounced rococo style, were produced in profusion during the period from 1759 to 1764. The well-known vases in the Jones bequest at the Victoria and Albert Museum, the two large examples in the British Museum, which must have been made in 1762,* the famous vases of similar kind formerly in the Dudley House collection, and the magnificent set of seven vases with claret ground in the possession of Lord Burton give us a most striking impression of the technical skill that had been reached. It is impossible to resist the feeling that Chelsea was matching itself against the factory of Sèvres, of which the French king had just become sole proprietor (1759). Extravagant and bizarre as the pieces of this kind generally are, setting at defiance every restriction that the material should have placed on the designer, with their pierced necks and covers, light scroll-work bases, and wildly interlacing handles, they remain as technical triumphs in the potter's art.

While in the pieces of the early period the influence of China, Japan, and Dresden is very noticeable, these later pieces are absolutely French in style. Subjects after Watteau, Boucher, and lesser French artists were painted in the panels of vases, often with considerable spirit and with a certain elegance of touch and taste.

* They were given to the British Museum 15th April, 1763.

Other vases painted with curious exotic birds, show how the " Chinoiserie " that affected French decorative art after the visit of the Chinese embassy to Louis XIV. was also making itself felt in England. The other productions of the factory shared in this change of spirit. The statuettes became larger, bolder, and more elaborate. The large figure of Britannia, and the figure of Una and the Lion (27 inches in height), George III. in Vandyke dress leaning on an altar, the elder Pitt (afterwards Earl of Chatham),* the Seasons, Cupids, shepherds and shepherdesses, actors and actresses, royal personages, military and naval commanders, and subjects from Greek and Roman mythology were mostly produced at this time ; in fact, an interesting volume might be written on the Chelsea figures and the sources from which they were derived. It has already been stated that many of them, both of the earlier and later period, were taken from contemporary engravings. The two white figures of Woodward as the " Fine Gentleman " and Kitty Clive as Mrs. Riot in Garrick's farce of *Lethe* (Figs. 11 and 13) are copied in this way from well-known engravings,† and are typical of a large group of Chelsea figures. The possibility that Bacon modelled for Chelsea has been already referred to, and we have direct evidence that Roubiliac, the sculptor, who lived in England from 1744 to 1762, modelled some of the figures and groups. The group called " The Music Lesson," a shepherd and shepherdess seated under a *bocage*, of which there is a magnificent specimen, elaborately coloured and gilt, in the Victoria and Albert Museum, is from his hand. It has been stated that some of the pieces made from his models have an " R " impressed in the paste, but many pieces that may safely be attributed to him have no such mark. Among these may be named the figures of " Shakespeare," " Apollo and the Muses," a " pair of figure groups, each consisting of two figures (male and female), and the whole representing the four seasons," as well as a group of " a man

* These pieces were made at various periods, and can often be approximately dated by the titles set forth in the scroll.

† Copies of these engravings are exhibited in the Ceramic Gallery, Victoria and Albert Museum.

PLATE VII.

Two late Chelsea Vases.

RAISED FLOWERS ON TURQUOISE GROUND.

British Museum.

(*See p.* 49.)

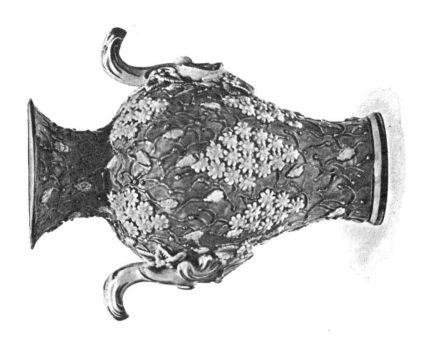

playing a hurdy-gurdy and a lady teaching a dog dressed as harlequin to dance."

It is necessary to draw attention here to the extraordinary use of raised flowers—*i.e.* flowers modelled in the round, in the decoration of Chelsea porcelain. The practice commenced in a very simple way in the earlier period with the modelling of foliage and flowers on the surface of the pieces—indeed, the goat and bee cream-jug exhibits something of this kind. Following the lead of Dresden, the Chelsea artists introduced festoons and wreaths of flowers on the shoulders of vases, or dropping over their handles and down their sides. Then little figures were produced with wreaths of flowers and foliage, and, finally, the fully developed boscage, or *bocage*, pieces, of which the "Music Lesson" already alluded to is the most wonderful example. A number of specimens of this "flowering" from its simpler to its most elaborate forms will be found on the pieces illustrated. Of the simplest type the elaborate late vase reproduced in colours on Plate VI. gives a very good illustration, showing both the way in which the flowers are modelled and the way in which they are frequently coloured. On Plate V. will be found two small scent bottles, one modelled in the form of a pink and the other as a little bouquet of stocks. These are fine examples of the high degree of skill attained by the china "flowerer." A third use of flowers is shown in the two vases of late Chelsea manufacture on Plate VII. In one vase the turquoise ground is sown all over with little porcelain flowers in white—a method also imitated from Dresden. Of course, the white star-like petals were put on the vase in the clay state, the piece was fired, and then glazed and fired again ; the soft turquoise enamel was then painted all over the ground, a task requiring great patience ; the stem and berries were touched in with green and red enamels, and the piece received its final fire. The companion vase on the same plate shows the more ordinary use of modelled flowering of the simplest type, although the ground colour proves that the piece cannot be earlier than about 1760. Fig. 2 gives a reproduction of one of the very elaborate *bocage*

E

pieces of later days. Similar candlesticks, modelled to illustrate the stories of La Fontaine's fables, are frequently referred to in the sale lists. The fable illustrated here is " The Vain Jackdaw." The final result is the production of a glittering porcelain toy, which has to be kept in a glass case to preserve it from destruction, and mainly noteworthy as an instance of misapplied ingenuity. In Fig. 14 will be found a group of flowers and leaves photographed from pieces in the process of manufacture, showing how these elaborate groups of flowers and leaves were built up from bits of clay shaped in the workman's hand, without the use of any mould, and put together with a little " slip."

The use of the rich grounds and lavish gilding of the late Chelsea period was not confined to cabinet pieces. We find frequent mention in the sale catalogues of dessert services, dessert plates, caudle cups with covers, chocolate cups with stands, and similar objects decorated with Mazarine blue, pea-green, and claret grounds, having reserved panels in white with elaborate paintings of figures, birds, and landscapes, enriched with heavy gilt borders. Of this kind was the famous dessert service mentioned by Horace Walpole in 1763, which was bought by the King and Queen, and presented to the Duke of Mecklenburg. This service cost £1,150. It had a Mazarine blue ground, and was richly decorated in gold. The Victoria and Albert Museum collection contains a number of richly decorated plates of this period. It is interesting to observe, where the gilding has been worn off, that the blue colour of the ground has run far beyond the rim and into the well of the plate. It was in order to hide this defect that the ornamental gold bands were made so broad ; otherwise, of course, the piece would have been quite unsaleable. In the catalogue of the last sale of Sprimont's productions which took place at Christie's, February 14th to 17th, 1770, Lot 70 of the last day's sale is thus described :—

" A very curious and matchless tea and coffee equipage, crimson and gold, most inimitably enamelled in figures from the designs of Watteau, consisting of twelve teacups with handles and saucers, six coffee ditto, teapot and stand, slop-bason, sugar-dish, and cream ewer."

FIG. 14.— ILLUSTRATIONS OF THE MANUFACTURE
OF CHINA FLOWERS.

MOORE, LONGTON.

This service sold for £43 1s., and it is evident from the special description given to it in the catalogue that such sets were rare. On Plate VIII. will be found reproductions of three pieces of a service identical with the one thus described. The pieces are portions of a magnificent service that has recently come to the Victoria and Albert Museum by bequest from the late Miss Emily S. Thomson, of Dover. The ground is of the famous claret colour, and of exceptionally beautiful tone, the gilding is most thickly applied, and is very finely chased, while the little figures in panels on the cups, cream ewer, and sugar basin, and on the bottoms of the saucers are not only charmingly conceived, but are drawn and painted with the utmost delicacy and skill. It would be impossible to close this account of the productions of Chelsea in the hands of Sprimont with a finer illustration of the excellence reached in its productions, in little more than twenty years.

It is necessary now, in order to make the sketch complete, that the history of the closing years of this important factory should be briefly recounted. As early as 1761 we find Sprimont stating in an advertisement that " As his indisposition will not permit him to carry on much longer, he takes the opportunity to assure the nobility, gentry, and others, that next year will be the last sale he will offer to the public." Again, in January, 1763, he states that " it will positively be his last sale, being unfortunately obliged on account of his illness to decline carrying on the same " ; and then follows a statement that he is about to dispose of the manufactory with the kilns, and so the advertisements run on almost like those of a "star" artist in our own day. Possibly there was no great production of Chelsea porcelain after 1764, but every effort was made to finish decorating all the best white pieces left on the works and in the warehouses. Sprimont actually retired from the concern in the autumn of 1769, when he disposed of the remainder of his lease of the premises, and of the kilns, grinding plant, models in wax and in lead, presses, and moulds, and all the materials, utensils, chattels, and effects to James Cox for the entirely insignificant sum of £600, thus proving that the Chelsea factory had never been a large one,* or that from 1764 it had gradually declined through neglect, until it was in a very poor condition indeed. In the early part of 1770 this same J. Cox transferred the business stock, moulds, kilns, and so forth, to Messrs. Duesbury and Co., proprietors of the Derby China Works, who paid him the sum of £612, together with £189 10s. for clay and tradesmen's bills for putting the warehouses and other buildings in repair.† This transaction seems to have been completed on the 9th February, 1770, and with the passing of the works into the hands of Duesbury and Co. a fresh period is entered upon which must, however, be treated separately. In 1770 the last sale of Sprimont's Chelsea porcelain took place at Christie's, and Sprimont himself died in 1771.

The first mark of the Chelsea porcelain was, as we have seen, the incised triangle, but this occurs on very few pieces, and it is probably either a workman's mark or a mark used when the factory was in its very early stages. During the period when the factory was really well known the mark appears to have been an anchor, applied in various forms. Much futile speculation has been wasted on conjectures as to the possible connection of this mark with the anchor on the Venetian porcelain. It has even been supposed that the Chelsea factory owed its rise to a company of Venetian glass-makers who settled in Chelsea under the patronage of the Duke of Buckingham in 1676. This glass-making venture had, however, been abandoned long before the period of Chelsea porcelain, and the Venetian porcelain of the eighteenth century seems to have been a poor imitation of Dresden porcelain, so that we can hardly look for any connection between that factory and Chelsea.

The earliest form of this Chelsea mark is in the shape of an embossed oval, bearing an anchor in low relief. This type of mark was always made separately, probably from a little stamp, and then stuck on to the piece. It generally occurs—as we should expect—

---

* Several different accounts put the number of workpeople at various times as about 100.

† This seems to be pretty strong evidence of the condition of decay into which this factory had fallen during its later years.

PLATE VIII.

Three Pieces of a late Chelsea Tea-service.

Bequeathed by Miss Emily S. Thomson to the Victoria and Albert Museum.

(*See pp.* 50-51.)

on figures, and particularly on the birds of the early period, though a few cups, bowls, and dishes also have this mark. Occasionally the embossed anchor has been touched in with enamel red colour. In later times the anchor was drawn by the enameller or gilder when he finished the decoration of the piece, and, as would be natural in such circumstances, it varies very much in style and size, and also in the colour used. Sometimes, though very seldom, it occurs in blue, but it is generally in red or in a brownish red colour—whichever, indeed, the enameller happened to be using. Only the gilder would be likely to make the mark in gold, and it is not surprising, therefore, to find that the pieces marked with the gold anchor are generally of a late period when lavish gilding had become such a feature of the decoration. Occasionally one finds two gold anchors side by side on these late pieces, and in a few exceptional cases the gold anchor actually occurs in full view among the ornamentation of the drapery of figures or on the scroll work of the stands.

Actual representations of typical Chelsea marks will be found in the section devoted to the marks of English porcelain.

CHAPTER VI.

DERBY—CHELSEA.

THE productions of the Chelsea factory, after it passed into the hands of Duesbury and Co. in 1770, have generally been considered along with those of Chelsea, under the name of Chelsea-Derby. There is no doubt that Duesbury continued to use some of the old Chelsea moulds, and doubtless produced many pieces that might easily be mistaken for genuine Chelsea productions. There is, however, a considerable number of existing pieces which can be referred without the slightest hesitation to this period, and they generally show some features so different from the productions of Sprimont, and at the same time have such definite Derby charac-teristics, that the term Derby-Chelsea seems a more appropriate one. In the description of the productions of Chelsea much has been said about the elaborate rococo style of the later pieces. The vases and ornamental figure groups produced after 1758–1759 were absolutely French in form and decoration. Duesbury, however, seems to have realised that the risks attending the production of such elaborate pieces as these were so great as to render them un-profitable. At all events, we find during the Derby-Chelsea period a great change in the shapes of the vases. They are, for the most part, mechanical copies of classic shapes somewhat resembling those with which Wedgwood was winning the applause of polite circles.* In the catalogue of the 1773 sale of the productions of Derby and Chelsea· Duesbury describes the ornamental pieces as " principally designs from the antique, representing tripods, altars, urns, vases, jars, etc." One cannot look on these productions with

* *See* p. 31.

FIGS. 15, 16, 17.—THREE VASES WITH
GOLD STRIPE DECORATION.
DERBY-CHELSEA.

a very favourable eye. The shapes were by no means adapted to production in porcelain—a material absolutely unknown to their original designers—neither can it be said that they lent themselves to the display of the qualities of the porcelain material, which from its nature seems to demand a lighter and more fanciful treatment· The one thing they had to offer to the china painter of the day was· a considerable area of plain space on the body of the vase, on which he could trace a medallion to receive an elaborate painting of landscape or figures. Occasionally, it is true, these pieces received a decoration which was not altogether out of harmony with the simplicity of their lines. The gold stripe decoration, which seems to be such a characteristic feature of many of the good Derby-Chelsea pieces, furnishes a case in point. The finely drawn thin gold lines improve rather than spoil the shapes, and form a pleasant diapering on their surface.

Figures 15, 16, and 17 give a representation of the three famous vases of this type in the British Museum, which illustrate all these points perfectly. The pieces are very well potted, the workmanship throughout being admirable of its kind ; but they are in the greatest contrast with the true Chelsea productions, and seem already to presage the spirit of mechanical excellence and artistic banality which was to come over English porcelain twenty years later.

Another famous Derby-Chelsea vase is reproduced in colours on Plate III. The specimen, which is in the Jones bequest in the Victoria and Albert Museum, shows the advancing influence of the taste for classic forms, though in this case the form has not been imitated directly from the antique, but from a Sèvres model. The introduction of handles in the shape of figures left in the biscuit state—*i.e.* not glazed—bespeaks the Derby influence, while the laboured decoration with which the piece is absolutely smothered is also eloquent of Derby and not of Chelsea.

This association of figures left in the biscuit or unglazed state (so that the finest of the modelled details should not be impaired by the coat of glaze), with supports and stands decorated in gold and colours, is frequently found in the productions of Derby-Chelsea. Biscuit figures are never mentioned in connection with the Chelsea sales, but in the 1773 sale of Derby-Chelsea attention is specially drawn to " Biscuit groups and single figures in great abundance, the subjects well chosen, and the modelling accurate." In the British Museum there is a statuette of George III., modelled after Zoffany, in which the figure is biscuit, while the stand and the classic urn against which the figure leans are glazed and decorated in blue and gold.* The statuette of " Catharine Macaulay " in the same collection is of a similar type.

There are numerous instances in which a copy of the same group occurs both in the biscuit condition, and also glazed and decorated. In the Schreiber collection there is a modelled group of three children disposed round an obelisk on a rock,† which is glazed and slightly coloured and gilt ; while in the same collection is a group similar to it in every respect—save that the obelisk is replaced by a tree, which is in the biscuit body.

It is difficult, or even impossible, to say whether certain pieces were produced at Chelsea or at Derby, and the mark when it occurs can be of little assistance in deciding such a question, for it was probably used at either factory indifferently during the period when both works were carried on by Duesbury. In Figs. 18, 19, and 20 will be found reproductions of three cups and saucers in the Franks collection which illustrate this difficulty. Two of the patterns (Figs. 18 and 20) are decorated in the slighter manner that is generally associated with the productions of Derby,‡ while the third (Fig. 19), which has a claret ground and rich gilding, is of a decidedly Chelsea character ; yet all the three pieces are marked with the Derby-Chelsea mark.

There are, of course, certain pieces which can be safely ascribed to the Chelsea factory, such as the " Cooper's bowl " in the Schreiber

---

* We learn from the sale list of 1774 that this figure was one of a group of three, representing the King, Queen, and Royal Family.

† This group is mentioned in the sale catalogue of 1771.

‡ Fig. 20 will be found in Haslem's " Old Derby China Factory," described as No. 11 in the Derby pattern book.

FIGS. 18, 19, 20.—THREE CUPS AND SAUCERS.
DERBY-CHELSEA.

collection. This piece is dated 1779, but a considerable exercise of imagination is needed to see any trace of " Chelsea " feeling in such a production, where careful and laboured workmanship is offered as a substitute for taste and elegance:

It will naturally be expected that some trace of the rich claret, pea-green, and turquoise colours so characteristic of the later Chelsea productions should be found on the Derby-Chelsea productions. The colours do occur on many pieces, but they are generally so thinly applied, or have been so diluted, that they seem the mere ghosts of their former selves. Many Derby-Chelsea figures could be cited in which these colours occur, but one example must suffice. In the Schreiber collection will be found a pair of little figures standing on roughly hewn rockwork bases, and supported by classic urns on pedestals. The figures are commonly known as Cupid and Psyche,* and their colouring is typical of a favourite Derby-Chelsea method. The pea-green and turquoise colours are used, but in irregularly disposed patches rather than as flat washes, and they are decidedly thin and poor in tone. The red colour, made from oxide of iron, is also used in a characteristic fashion ; it is washed on very thinly over the rockwork bases, and is consequently so pale as to become almost of a salmon hue. In other figures a flesh tint is obtained by a thin wash of this red colour all over the exposed parts of figures,† a custom absolutely unknown at Chelsea in its palmy days.

Duesbury carried on the old Chelsea factory from the beginning of 1770 to 1773, when the original lease of Sprimont ran out. He then leased it for a period of seven years, which ended in 1780. Apparently the difficulties of carrying on two factories so widely separated as Derby and Chelsea—especially having regard to the means of communication existing 120 years ago—had begun to make themselves felt, for the next lease was only for one year. In 1781 the premises were leased for three more years, and

---

* Sir A. W. Franks, however, pointed out that the attributes of the female figure were rather those of " Hygeia " than of " Psyche."

† *See* figure of a " Triton " in the Schreiber collection (Victoria and Albert Museum).

finally in 1784 the old Chelsea factory was closed in fact as well as in spirit.   The kilns and workshops were demolished, the moulds broken up or removed to Derby, and some of the old Chelsea workmen who still remained in Duesbury's service settled in Derby.

The mark of the productions during this period, when any mark occurs, is the anchor of Chelsea combined with the " D " of Derby ; but, as has been already mentioned, it is difficult to assign pieces bearing this mark definitely to the Chelsea factory.   For reproductions of actual marks of this period the reader is referred to the Section on Marks.

CHAPTER VII.

BOW.

DESPITE the labours of many careful students and writers, the early history of the porcelain factory at Stratford-le-Bow is by no means clear. One school of writers, without adducing any facts in support of such a date, places its foundation as early as 1730 ; while another school sees the origin of the works in a patent granted to Edward Heylin, of Bow, and Thomas Frye, of West Ham, in 1745,* for the production of porcelain from " an earth the produce of the Chirokee nation in America, called by the natives ' unaker,' " and a glass or frit formed by melting together sand and potash. There is no information how these two men, one of whom is described as a merchant and the other as a painter, came to know of the existence of china clay (the " unaker " of the patent). Neither has it occurred to anyone to enquire whether it would be possible to make a porcelain in the manner and of the materials specified. Possibly the description given is purposely vague, but there can be no doubt that porcelain was never made in any quantity under this patent.† The most probable explanation is that Heylin and Frye became acquainted in some way with the adventurous traveller who first brought the Cherokee clay to England, having recognised its similarity to the kaolin of the Chinese.‡ This man appears to have had some pieces made from his clay, and he may have entered into an agreement with Heylin and Frye to supply

* The patent was applied for cn December 6th, 1744 ; the specification was enrolled April 5th, 1745.

† See p. 10.

‡ Wm. Cookworthy, the founder of the Plymouth factory, had some relations with this man in 1745.

them with his material. The wording of the patent clearly shows that they wished to preserve the use of this "unaker" to themselves, but the clay never came to this country in any quantity, and though we hear of it again at intervals for nearly twenty years, it is only as a wonderful material from which porcelain was to be made if it could be obtained in sufficient quantity. Nothing is known of any factory belonging to Heylin and Frye, and it can only be surmised that they may have spent some years in trying to make porcelain after the manner set forth in this patent, and with the substitution of some other form of clay for the "unaker." If such were the case, they must soon have found that the potash glass described in their patent was also useless for such a purpose, and they would be plunged into a sea of experiments. In 1749 Frye took out another patent for the production of porcelain from totally different materials.* The wording of the earlier patent is clearness itself compared with that of the later. The marvellous substance to be protected this time was a certain "virgin earth," produced by calcining animals, vegetables, and fossils, and particularly "all animal substances, all fossils of the calcareous kind, as chalk, limestone, etc." This "virgin earth," after washing and grinding, was to be mixed with flint (white pebble, or clear sand), and made up into a paste with water. This paste was to be shaped into balls or bricks and burned in a fierce fire; it was then to be finely ground again, and made into a working paste by the addition of one-third of its weight of pipe-clay. It has been stated very definitely that this "virgin earth" was bone-ash, but from the specification it might just as well have been lime—and, indeed, it is very probable that Frye was unable to distinguish clearly between the bone-ash obtained by calcining animal substances and the lime obtained by calcining "fossils of the calcareous kind, as chalk, limestone, etc." It may be said at once that it would be possible to make porcelain in this way, using either bone-ash or lime, but the ware would be of such a tender description and so

---

* This patent was applied for on November 17th, 1748, and the specification enrolled March 17th, 1749.

PLATE IX.

Bow Inkstand,

With Inscription, "Made at New Canton, 1750."

(*See p.* 61.)

Craft Bowl.

British Museum.

(*See p.* 68.)

apt to fly to pieces, that without considerable modification it is impossible to regard this patent as a very practical one, or one likely to have formed the basis of an extensive manufacture. Professor Church has proved by numerous analyses that many pieces of Bow porcelain contain bone-ash, but there is some uncertainty as to their date. For the reason given above, as well as from the quality of many Bow pieces produced after 1750, it is impossible to see in either of the patents anything but imperfectly developed ideas.

The first definite information we have of a factory at Bow comes from certain memorandum books, diaries, and notebooks formerly in the possession of Lady Charlotte Schreiber, and written by a John Bowcocke, who was a commercial manager and traveller of the works. From these books it appears that the Bow works belonged to Messrs. Crowther and Weatherby, who entered into partnership in 1750, and that Thomas Frye was employed as works manager. We are also informed that the works was called "New Canton," and this statement, which is confirmed from other sources, is of the utmost importance, as it serves to identify a number of dated pieces, which fix the nature of the body and glaze made at this period. These are certain small inkstands (one of which is reproduced on Plate IX.), which bear the painted legend, "Made at New Canton, 1750." * These little pieces furnish a definite standard by which we may judge how the ware was made, and they also show the early use of the "Prunus" design, which was such a favourite device of the Bow decorators in later days. The paste of these pieces is not very white or very transparent, and the glaze, which is yellowish in tint, is particularly soft and luscious-looking. The glaze might conceivably have been made after the manner described in Frye's patent of 1749. The body, however, is not a bone body, but evidently a glassy porcelain of the same type as the early Chelsea. Many of the best Bow pieces are of this same quality,

---

* Other specimens are similarly marked, " Made at New Canton, 1751," and we know that they continued to be sold as late as 1757.

and, with their soft rich paste and glaze, have a very different appearance from the later Bow pieces. In the British Museum collection there are three dated pieces which serve to fix the appearance of the body and glaze at different periods of the factory's history. First, there is the inkstand already mentioned, which is dated 1750; second, the Craft bowl, which was made in 1760; third, a plate inscribed on the back in underglaze blue, "Mr. Robert Crowther, Stockport, Cheshire, 1770." It is curious that these three pieces should be dated 1750, 1760, 1770; but the first piece is of the richest body and glaze, while the last piece is altogether whiter and poorer in appearance, the Craft bowl being of intermediate quality. In this factory, as at Chelsea and elsewhere, the early glassy body was probably found too costly for general use because of the heavy losses in firing, and by the gradual introduction of mixtures on the lines of Frye's patent of 1749, the commercial working of the undertaking was rendered more constant and secure. It would be as unwise as it is impossible to fix any definite date for the introduction of the different bodies and glazes, for it is almost certain that different bodies were in use for various pieces produced at the same time; much trouble will, however, be saved to collectors and others if they will look upon the Bow body and glaze as varying from time to time within fairly wide limits, while an examination of the three pieces mentioned shows how strongly marked the differences can be.

Returning to the history of the factory, it is known that Frye remained as manager till 1759, when he retired from the business owing to ill-health.* In 1753 a warehouse for the sale of the productions of the factory was opened near the Royal Exchange in Cornhill. In 1757 what is believed to have been the first public sale by auction of the productions of the factory was held at the auction rooms of Cock and Co., "in Spring Gardens, leading into St. James's Park." Later in the same year (1757), a West-End warehouse was opened. An

* For a fuller account of the history of this interesting man reference may be made to Chaffers' "Marks and Monograms."

advertisement of that year states : " For the convenience of the nobility and gentry, their warehouse on the Terrace in St. James's Street is constantly supplied with everything new, where it is sold as at Cornhill, with the real Price marked on each piece without Abatement." This second warehouse does not appear to have answered expectations, for it was abandoned in the very next year (1758), and the entire stock housed in it was sold by auction. In 1762 Weatherby died, and the remaining partner, Crowther, became bankrupt in 1763. The stock-in-trade of the factory was sold by auction in May, 1764. Nothing is said of the sale of the business or the buildings, however, and Crowther seems to have carried on the works, probably on a reduced scale, for several years longer. There are the plates already mentioned, marked " Robt. Crowther, 1770," and probably made for some relative, as evidence in this direction ; and also the statement in the London Directory (1770–1775) that John Crowther, of the Bow China Works, had a warehouse at 28, St. Paul's Churchyard. The business, however, could not have been a lucrative one in its latter days, for in 1775, or 1776, it was sold to Duesbury for an insignificant sum ; the moulds and implements were transferred to Derby ; and in the following year, March 20th, 1777, Crowther was elected an inmate of Morden College, Blackheath, where he was still alive in 1790.*

Considerable light has been thrown on the productions of the factory by the notes in the memorandum books of Bowcocke already alluded to ; by the bowl in the British Museum and the memorandum written by its painter, T. Craft, in 1790 ; by an interesting find of fragments of porcelain and moulds, evidently on the forgotten site of the works, during some drainage operations in 1868 at the match factory of Messrs. Bell and Black at Bell Road, St. Leonard's Street, Bromley-by-Bow ; and, finally, by the researches of Mr. Nightingale. From these various sources much information has been gathered as to the nature of the pieces, the favourite styles of decoration, and the methods of carrying on the business. At the outset, or, at all

* *See* memorandum of T. Craft in the British Museum.

events, at the earliest period for which we have documentary evidence, efforts were steadily devoted to the production of " useful," as opposed to ornamental, articles. Thus, in the notice of the first public sale by auction of Bow porcelain (1757) mention is made of " a large assortment of the most useful china in Lots, for the use of Gentlemen's kitchens, Private families, Taverns, etc." No such references occur in the sale lists or advertisements of the Chelsea factory, and there can be little doubt that this marks a real distinction in the manner in which the two factories were conducted, though both were bidding for the support of the London public. At Chelsea the productions were largely of an ornamental character ; the works does not seem in its busiest time to have found employment for more than a hundred workpeople or so ; and Sprimont speaks with pride of the sales having reached the sum of £3,500 during the winter of 1752–53. The memorandum of T. Craft in the British Museum states that the Bow factory employed between two and three hundred workpeople ; and Bowcocke's account-book gives the amount of cash received as being over £10,000 in the year 1753. The Chelsea factory seems to have relied on its annual sales by auction, together with the regular sales from the warehouse, to dispose of its productions. We find, on the other hand, that Bowcocke took country journeys to extend the sales of Bow. During the year 1758, for instance, he spent eight months in Dublin receiving consignments of goods from the works and selling them by auction. The information in Bowcocke's books, however, which is of the greatest interest at the present time, is that which throws light on the actual productions of the factory. This information, as well as that derived from the find of waste fragments already referred to, has cleared up many doubtful points as to the *provenance* of whole groups of pieces. Formerly collectors were too much in the habit of attributing all the good pieces to Chelsea or to Bow, according to their personal predilection. Now, however, there are so many pieces whose origin cannot be doubted, that a study of their technical and artistic characteristics furnishes almost a set of rules by which these earlier attributions can be checked, and, if needful, corrected. There will always remain certain pieces, however, which appear to have been made from practically identical moulds at both factories. The fine figures of " Kitty Clive " and " Woodward," illustrated in connection with the Chelsea factory, and the " figure of Britannia with a medallion " bearing the portrait of George II.," illustrated in Fig. 1, are well known cases in point. The actual pieces from which the illustrations are taken were probably made as stated here, the first two at Chelsea and the last at Bow; but there are other copies of the same figures in existence that seem to have originated from the rival factory. It is certain that Chelsea pieces were copied at the Bow factory, for mention of Chelsea pieces taken or sent to Bow occurs several times in Bow-cocke's books, and it is equally possible that some of the Bow pieces may have been reproduced at Chelsea. When both factories were busily engaged in copying Oriental and Continental pieces it is hardly likely that they would refrain from copying from each other, especially in the case of pieces designed to satisfy a temporary " rage " for some favourite actor or actress of the day.

The use of the " Prunus " decoration on the earliest known pieces of Bow porcelain (*see* Plate IX.) has already been referred to. The early productions seem to have been very largely influenced—at all events, so far as the decoration was concerned—by Oriental examples ; and, indeed, one or two decorative ideas derived from such sources formed the stock-in-trade of the designers and decorators through a considerable period of the factory's history. It cannot be safely said that the simpler forms of blue and white porcelain were produced first, because these earliest known pieces are in colours ; but certainly blue and white pieces were produced in quantity almost from the beginning. An illustration of a Bow mug decorated with a spirited drawing of a dragon in underglaze blue is given on Plate II., and many pieces similarly decorated with patterns painted in blue occur in all good collections. Some of these blue painted pieces bear a monogram of " T " and " F " combined, which probably indicates that such pieces

F

were painted by Thomas Frye himself, and as Frye retired from the works in 1759 it may be reasonably assumed that such pieces were made before that date.

The little teapot (Fig. 22) in the British Museum is thus marked, and with the delicate flutings of the body, the simple embossed vine ornament left white, and the painting of bamboo in pale greyish blue colour, it forms as charming an example of the fine artistic quality often shown in the work of this class as could be desired. Frye was an artist of some repute, and in pieces such as these the artistic perception of the qualities of the material is very evident. In Bowcocke's books during the period from 1750–1758 frequent entries relate to patterns in blue and white, and among the fragments found on the site of the old works a large proportion were of this class (*see* Fig. 23), so that the production of blue and white pieces must be regarded as one of the most constant features of the business, and as a proof that the works largely depended for its success on the sale of " useful " articles. Occasionally large and important blue and white pieces are met with, such as the hexagonal vases with foliage and birds painted in the Chinese manner, of which there are fine examples in the Schreiber collection. It should be said that the blue of the Bow porcelain, like that of Chelsea and of early Worcester, is much greyer and softer in tone than the blue of modern productions ; the glaze, too, is often slightly " tinted," and the general effect of the blue and white is consequently harmonious and pleasing. Of course, in a factory where the body and glaze varied so much as at Bow, it is impossible to speak of any particular shade of blue as typical, but the painted mug (Plate II.) is a good example of a large class of such pieces.

In all the documents relating to the factory, there are frequent references to Japanese patterns. Thus, in the sale lists, mention is often made of " the old brown-edged Japan pattern," and it is stated that these pieces were " most beautifully painted by several of the finest masters from Dresden." It is barely possible that painters from Dresden can have been employed at Bow and although this very class of Japanese design was largely

Fig. 21.—CUP AND SAUCER, EMBOSSED
PINE CONE ORNAMENT AND
GREEN BAND.
BOW.

Fig. 22.—BLUE AND WHITE TEAPOT
(MARKED T.F.).
BOW.

copied at Dresden, the Bow painters probably got their ideas from actual Japanese pieces. In the notebooks of the works several entries relate to the loan of Japanese pieces by patrons of the factory, in order that copies might be made for them. Under date May 28th, 1756, the following entry occurs :—

" Patterns received from Lady Cavendish : a Japan octagon cup and saucer, lady pattern; a rib'd and scollop'd cup and saucer, image pattern ; a basket bordered dessart (dessert ?) plate ; a Japan bread and butter plate."

We know that patterns were frequently furnished in this way to most of the eighteenth century factories, and among them would undoubtedly come some of the Kakiyemon pieces which the Dutch had imported into Europe in quantities. In a previous chapter * mention has been made of the influence that these designs had on the productions of the early English factories, and nowhere was this influence more strongly marked than at Bow. Octagonal dishes and plates, scallop-shaped dishes, cups and saucers, were produced, with the edge lined in brown, an ornamental foliage border inside this in bright iron red, and then in the centre of the piece a slight design generally of a branch of prunus in flower. In addition to this, we often find a couple of small birds, which might be called quails or partridge, a wheatsheaf, a simple growing plant, or some star-shaped flowers in red and gold scattered about the piece. Designs of this kind make up the varied forms which the Japanese patterns suggested to the English painters. The painting is all executed on the glaze in red, relieved with a few touches of green, and brightened with the rich dead gilding of early days. The earliest pieces are undoubtedly those with the brown lined rim, which were specially mentioned in the sale list of 1758. These pieces are often extremely clumsy in make, the bottoms of the dishes and plates being sometimes two or three times as thick as the sides, so that it is wonderful how they stood the ordeal of repeated firings at all. Where it is thick the ware is absolutely opaque, but in thinner parts it is translucent enough, and has a

* *See* p. 27.

decidedly creamy tint. The glaze is obviously very rich in lead, for it has a pale yellow tint, particularly where it has gathered thickly, and, having consequently been slightly decomposed by the action of moist air in the hundred and fifty years or so that the pieces have been in existence, is often slightly iridescent. The later pieces, obviously made from a different composition, are thinner, better potted, and also whiter in tone, so that the effect of the red and gold decoration is not quite so harmonious and pleasing. In these later pieces the brown edge disappears, and the red border of painted leafage becomes more elaborate. Other colours are also introduced, and we get, in addition to red, green, and gold, touches of yellow and blue, but all painted over the glaze.

By 1760 the designs had also been elaborated and removed further from the Japanese originals. The Craft bowl which is reproduced in colours on Plate IX. was painted in this year. Craft tells us in his memorandum that :

"It is painted in what we used to call the old Japan taste, a taste at that time much esteemed by the then Duke of Argyle ; * there is nearly two pennyweight of gold—about 15 shillings ; I had it in hand, at different times, about three months ; about two weeks' time was bestowed upon it ; it could not have been manufactured &c. for less than £4. There is not its similitude. I took it in a box to Kentish Town, and had it † burned there in Mr. Gyles's kiln, cost me 3s. ; it was cracked the first time of using it."

But for Craft's statement it would have been difficult to see any trace of Japanese influence in the ornament on the bowl. The decoration consists of festoons or swags of flowers and leaves, with loose pendant scrolls between—a device never used by the Japanese. The piece is evidently one in which Craft, working for himself, has carried out some of his own notions, and the only echo of the far-off original idea is the rich red and gold, which give the colour note, even though touches of yellow, green, and a pale slaty blue are also used. There are many pieces in existence which have been identified as the productions of Bow by their

* This must have been the third Duke of Argyle, who commanded the Royalist army at Sherrifmuir in 1715. He died suddenly in 1761.

† That is, the painting which is over the glaze.

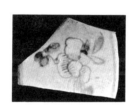

Fig. 23.—A MOULD AND FOUR
FRAGMENTS OF PORCELAIN.
BOW.

resemblance in style to this Craft bowl. For instance, the plate in the Schreiber collection figured in Church's " English Porcelain " has a similar arrangement of festoons forming a border, but the centre has a design of two fighting cocks which is perfectly Oriental in style.

In the memorandum books of Bowcocke, frequent mention is made of " sprigged " cups, boats, and tureens, as early as 1752. These are the pieces, generally in white, which are decorated with modelled ornament, separately made in a mould, and then stuck on the piece while it was in the clay state. An illustration of this simple form of ornament is given in Fig. 4 c., and a Chinese piece is also reproduced in Fig. 4 D for comparison. The " Prunus " pattern was largely used for this method of ornamentation, but other and less distinctively Oriental forms were also employed. Fortunately, among the fragments unearthed in 1868 about a dozen of the small moulds used for this purpose were found. In Fig. 23 will be found a reproduction of a few fragments of the find preserved in the Victoria and Albert Museum. The lower illustration is from one of these moulds. In use, the workman squeezed a little flattened roll of clay into such a mould with his thumb ; the superfluous clay was cleanly and sharply scraped off, and with a little careful handling the " press " could then be removed from the mould and attached with a little thin " slip " of clay and water to the object to be decorated, while it was still in the clay state. On firing the applied ornament became fused to the body of the piece so firmly that it is impossible to see any line of junction. Ornament applied in this way is always spoken of by potters as " sprigged," so that there can be no doubt as to the pieces indicated by that title in the old work books.

In addition to the moulds and sprigged pieces, attention must be drawn to the knife handles decorated with rather heavy rococo and strap-work scrolls. One of these is figured among the fragments, so that a trade in these little articles probably continued down to the closing days of the works. The modelling on the knife handles was often heightened by the application of touches of underglaze blue colour, and elaborate specimens occur in which overglaze colour and gold have been subsequently applied, but these latter pieces are rare.

Statuettes and groups of figures were produced at Bow probably throughout the whole period of its history, and though they were not so numerous or so important as those of Chelsea, they are deserving of careful attention. Speaking generally, the Bow figures were neither so well modelled in the first place, nor so well " stuck up " by the potter as the Chelsea figures ; and as certain differences of treatment in the enamelling are also found, there is less difficulty in separating the figures of one factory from those of the other than has been generally supposed. The advertisement of 1753 emanating from this factory : " A Person is wanted who can model small figures in clay neatly," apparently indicates that no great progress had been made in this department at that date. What are commonly supposed to be the earliest Bow figures are certain small pieces in white, which are certainly rather elementary both in style and manufacture. Generally these earliest figures are on perfectly simple flat stands, which are, indeed, nothing more than little square or round cakes of clay. (*See* Fig. 27.) The figures are seldom more than four or five inches high, and it is readily seen by the way in which they are built up and supported that they are tentative efforts. The well-known figures of an actor and actress in costume, the most striking feature of which is a heavy fur cloak thrown back and hanging down behind the figure, are typical early pieces. The fur cloak is really a piece of clay modelled by hand and applied to the figure, which it serves at once to support and to attach firmly to the simple flat base.

A most interesting study might be made of what may be described as the " construction " of porcelain figures. The way in which the figures are supported by rocks, tree-trunks, and other accessories, so that they may go through the fiery ordeal of the furnace without being entirely warped out of shape, varies

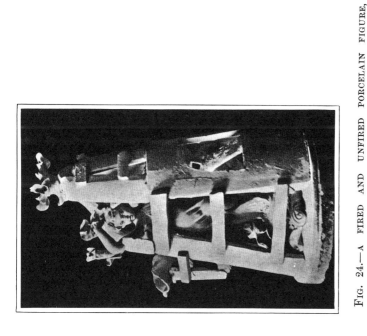

FIG. 24.—A FIRED AND UNFIRED PORCELAIN FIGURE, MADE FROM THE SAME MOULD, SHOWING THE SHRINKING DUE TO FIRING, AND THE ELABORATE "PROPPING" NEEDED TO KEEP THE FIGURE TRUE.

MOORE; LONGTON.

from time to time and from factory to factory. The making of the figure is a most elaborate process, for in most cases the body of the figure, the limbs, and the head, must all be moulded separately, and then " stuck up," or united by the application of a thin " slip " of clay and water. This serves to hold the pieces together temporarily, very much as a wooden figure might be held together with glue ; but, of course, when the piece is fired the parts unite by fusion into a perfect whole. The actual figure-making— *i.e.* the moulding and " sticking up " of the parts—is a most important part of the process. However skilfully or artistically the original modelling of the figure may have been executed, its character is either preserved or destroyed at this stage. As a rule the Bow figures were not nearly so well carried out as those of Chelsea, Derby, and Bristol. Everyone is by this time acquainted with the fact that porcelain shrinks largely in the drying and firing, and the greatest care has to be taken to support the pieces during the firing to prevent distortion and warping. In figures this is especially the case, and in addition to using accessories such as trees, rocks, or dresses to support the figure, an elaborate scaffolding of props has to be erected round a porcelain figure before it can be fired in safety. These separate props must be of the same porcelain material as the figure itself, so that they may shrink at exactly the same rate. They are, of course, not attached to the piece, and a little powdered flint is dusted over the parts where they touch the figure to prevent any adhesion. In Fig. 24 will be found an illustration from a photograph of a fired and an unfired porcelain figure made from the same mould. The unfired figure is surrounded with the scaffolding and supported at various points by props, and the necessity for such support is emphasised by the difference in size between the " unfired " and the " fired " figure.

Among the early Bow figures the best known are the figures of actor and actress already alluded to, harlequin, pierrot, Dutch dancers, male and female cooks, man with bag-pipes, a sphinx with the head of Peg Woffington, the famous actress, and small figures representing the four seasons and the four continents. The simple flat stands of the earlier pieces were soon replaced by more elaborate stands, designed in the favourite rococo style of the period ; but there is this general distinction between the stands of the Bow figures and those of the Chelsea figures, that the scrolls of the former are generally prolonged into unmistakable little feet at the corners, while the stands of the latter are almost invariably lower and flatter, having their bases raised very little. The Bow stands are neither so well shaped nor so nicely proportioned as those of Chelsea, and they are sometimes formed in two tiers—a practice which does not seem to have been followed at Chelsea. This will be seen by comparing the Chelsea figures illustrated in this book with the figures of the girl and boy (Figs. 25 and 26). In the Schreiber collection the figure of the actor with a fur cloak, already named, occurs in two forms, one evidently later than the other. In the earlier form the stand is a simple cake of clay, but in the later the stand is an elaborate scroll base raised on feet. A few of the Bow figures, as has been said,* are with great probability attributed to the sculptor, John Bacon (1740–99). Of these the best known are the male and female cooks, one of which is illustrated in Fig. 27. These delicately modelled little pieces, often found in white, are sometimes marked with an impressed " B " at the back of the stands. † The largest figure supposed to have been made at Bow is a copy of the " Farnese Flora," 18¼ inches high, and the modelling of this is also attributed to Bacon. A specimen of this large figure will be found in the Schreiber collection.

The enamelling of the figures at Bow never seems to have been done so tastefully as at Chelsea, and certain of the colours used often serve to distinguish the work of one factory from that of the other, in default of other evidence. At Chelsea, for instance, the rich blue, pea-green, and turquoise were often used on the later figures ; and though some attempts were made at Bow to obtain similar colours, they were not entirely successful. There are,

* *See* p. 44.   † *See* the Section on Marks.

Fig. 27. A COOK (ATTRIBUTED TO JOHN BACON).
BOW.

Fig. 26.—FIFER. **BOW.**

Fig. 25.—SHEPHERDESS.
BOW.

however, three colours largely used at Bow in the decoration of figures which are almost distinctive of the factory. The first of these is an enamel sealing-wax red, made from oxide of iron, which is so badly compounded that it is often quite dry and wanting in gloss. An excellent example of the use of this colour will be found on a small statuette of " Europe " in the British Museum. The second colour is a cold opaque enamel blue of quite unpleasant tone, which is often used for touching up parts of the dresses. It is of varying quality, but in the Schreiber collection are two figures — the Marquis of Granby and General Wolfe—upon which it is used at full strength. A third colour is a gold purple which, when strong (as in the same figures), is barely tolerable ; in thin washes it is distinctly unpleasant, as it becomes of a pale mauve-pink hue. The use of this purple and pinkish enamel was, of course, not confined to Bow, but the exact tint produced on many of the Bow pieces is colder and more inharmonious than that of most of the pieces made elsewhere. The difference between the enamelling at Bow and at Chelsea is shown by such a trifling detail as the colouring of the faces of figures. At Bow a little dab of iron-red was put in the middle of the cheek, and was considered all-sufficient. At Chelsea this little dab of red has been softened off and stippled down to the white with the greatest care and nicety. It is by the observation of such apparently insignificant details that the collector can distinguish between the productions of the two factories. In addition to these statuettes, little figures on stands, with *bocages,* and nozzles for candlesticks, were also produced at Bow, but they were generally smaller and less elaborate than the Chelsea candlesticks. It is said that the occurrence of a square hole at the back of the stands or bases of these figures is distinctive of the Bow pieces.

The use of printing at Bow also deserves attention. In Bowcocke's notebooks mention of " printed " ware occurs as early as 1756, and many pieces are in existence which go to prove that printing was extensively used there—another point of difference between Bow and Chelsea. It has been suggested that Bow pieces were sent to Liverpool to be printed by Sadler and Green, but there seems no reason to suppose that such a troublesome and expensive course would be pursued, when the success of printing as applied to Battersea enamel had attracted much notice in London before the experiments of Sadler and Green had ever been heard of, even in Liverpool. The actual printing on the extant Bow pieces is so different, too, from the early work of the Liverpool printers that it is difficult to suppose there can be any connection between them. Generally speaking, the Bow printing is in the fine line work similar to the piece reproduced in Fig. 28. This design—known as " Hancock's tea party "—will be more fully described elsewhere ; * it will suffice to say here that it was the work of Hancock, who was an engraver at Battersea, and afterwards at Worcester. Presumably, he engraved this plate either while he was at Battersea or before he went to Worcester. It is obvious that when this piece was produced at Bow the process of printing was regarded as a wonderful one, for while the centre of the plate is printed, the border has been painted in by hand, in the well known Bow-Japan style. Among the most characteristic productions of Bow in which printing played a part are the pieces of table ware, with houses and groups of people of a pronounced Chinese type printed in outline and then washed in with strong and rather crude enamel colours—purple, yellow, blue, and green. A third type of printed ornament occurs in the decoration of the robe and the stand of the large figure of Britannia in the British Museum (see Fig. 1). The floral sprays on the dress, and the little scene on the base supporting the figure, have printed outlines and have then been carefully touched in with colour.

Many marks have been attributed to Bow, but of these the only ones that need be mentioned here are the anchor and dagger, generally painted in red or a reddish brown. The anchor may have been imitated from Chelsea, and it has been suggested that, as Crowther and Weatherby were both freemen of the City of London, the dagger was taken from the City arms. An

* See pp. 105 and 107.

FIG. 28 —PLATE WITH TRANSFER PRINT
("HANCOCK'S TEA PARTY").
BOW.

arrow, with or without an annulet, is occasionally found ; but the Caduceus and the bow and arrow marks are very doubtful. The monogram of Frye which occurs on a number of pieces has been already referred to. Actual examples of marks are given in the appendix, but it must be stated that the majority of Bow pieces are unmarked, and many marks generally given for Bow are of doubtful significance.

CHAPTER VIII.

THE story of the early porcelain factory at Longton Hall, Staffordshire, is soon told, for it was in-existence only a few years (1752–58), and its productions never really reached the conditions of a perfected manufacture. Many writers have seen, in the few advertisements of the wares of this factory collected by Mr. Nightingale, the record of two separate ventures, but there seems no real ground for such an assumption. The name of William Littler occurs in almost every published notice that has been unearthed, and as he was a salt-glaze potter of some repute, we have certain information about him altogether apart from his connection with the porcelain works. Shaw, the assiduous collector of the gossip of the Potteries, gives a short account of him, and as his information was probably obtained from old workmen who had known Littler, it is worth while to summarise his statements here.

William Littler and his brother-in-law Aaron Wedgwood first introduced the use of Cobalt in the manufacture of Staffs. salt-glazed ware.*

If this be true, then Littler helped to produce the first blue salt-glazed pieces—a fact which might help to account for the bright blue used at Longton Hall.

From his success with salt-glaze he was led to attempt the production of porcelain. He left Brownhills near Tunstall and removed to Longton Hall where he achieved considerable success; but owing to the lack of demand for this kind of ware, he lost all his money in the venture and finally discontinued it.

* Shaw's " History of the Rise and Progress of the Staffs. Potteries," pp. 168 and 198.

He goes on to say that—

the porcelain was a fritt body ; that it was fired with wood because it would not bear coals ;* and that its defect was inability to bear sudden or excessive changes of temperature. The specimens which are well calculated to deceive the eye of the spectators are cylindrical cups, with handles showing some taste, a tolerable glaze, and enamelled with flowers ; but there are many specks, and the whole has a greyish hue, yet they are calculated to surprise his fellows by their similarity to foreign porcelain in body, glaze, shapes and enamelling.

The information thus summarised is sufficiently accurate in its main outlines, even though the date given (1765) is absolutely wrong. Of how many potters during the eighteenth century might a similar story have been told ? An enthusiastic attempt to produce porcelain, a few years of struggle, partial successes alternating with disastrous failure ; the exhaustion of resources, and, finally, of hope itself, and then a return to the ranks as a journeyman or manager at some more successfully conducted works.

How Littler was really led to commence his experiments in this direction will probably never be known. But the resemblance between the body and glaze of Longton Hall and those of Chelsea is very great ; the style and shapes of many of the pieces of the former have a very strong family likeness to the early leaf-dishes and vases of the latter ; and, finally, it is only on Chelsea porcelain and on that of Longton Hall that we find a splendid under-glaze blue colour lavishly used as a groundwork on ornamental pieces at this early date. Thus it is difficult to arrive at any other conclusion than that Littler had either worked at Chelsea himself or had derived a considerable amount of information from some expert potter who had competent knowledge of what was going on there.†

---

* On this point also *see* Cookworthy's statement concerning Plymouth porcelain, p. 125.

† It is possible, of course, but hardly probable, that he may have learnt something from the Staffordshire workmen already alluded to (*see* p. 34) after their return from Chelsea, and, obtaining from them some general ideas and perhaps a few odd pieces of the ware, worked out the rest for himself.

However this may be, he had produced something saleable by 1752, for in that year advertisements appeared in *Aris's Birmingham Gazette*, acquainting the public with the fact that Littler and Co., at Longton Hall, Staffordshire, were prepared to supply ornamental porcelain or china ware, either wholesale or retail, on application at the works. As to the pieces actually produced at this early period there is absolutely no information, but in all probability the factory was carried on in a very humble way, and its products were sold in the Midland districts, where Littler and his fellow-potters of Staffordshire had long been accustomed to dispose of their wares. Nothing further is known of the factory until 1757, when a sale of Longton Hall porcelain was advertised to take place in London. Littler had no doubt learnt of the Chelsea and Bow sales by auction that had taken place in the capital, and looked upon a London auction sale as the best means of extending the vogue of his porcelain, which by this time had doubtless been greatly improved. The first actual description of the articles produced is found in this advertisement, where mention is made of "tureens, covers and dishes, large cups and covers, jars and beakers, leaf basons and plates, melons, colliflowers, elegant epargnes, and other ornamental and useful porcelain both white and enamelled." The sale apparently did not answer expectations, as it was never repeated ; and, judging by the pieces that remain in collections, this is not remarkable, for the ware must have compared very unfavourably in the eyes of the London public with the better made and more tastefully decorated productions of Chelsea and Bow. At all events, the advertisements of the factory (with the name of Littler) again appear in *Aris's Birmingham Gazette* during 1757, and finally in 1758, after which the factory is heard of no more. Tradition says that it passed into the possession of Duesbury of Derby, and was absorbed into his factory, but the statement presumably means that Duesbury purchased and removed the stock and moulds, not that he took over the business as a going concern.

It has been generally stated that Duesbury was actively con-

Cupids and Goat.

Bowl and Cover formed of overlapping Leaves.

Franks Collection : British Museum.

(See p. 80.)

cerned in this factory about 1754–56, but there seems little direct evidence to support this view, except that in two legal documents of 1755 Duesbury is described as of Longton Hall, enameller. It is known that Duesbury's father, who was a currier, was living near Longton Hall, and when Duesbury, having long worked as an enameller and employer of enamellers in London, became ambitious to manufacture as well as to decorate porcelain, he may have turned to that factory as one where he would be likely to obtain a partnership on easy terms. If such a scheme was ever contemplated, it can hardly have been carried to any practical issue, for Duesbury was in London until 1754, at all events, and in the autumn of 1755 he must have been making arrangements to go to Derby, as he removed thither in the January of 1756.*

The actual pieces of porcelain attributed to Longton Hall are precisely of the kind to be expected from what has already been said. In some respects very striking in colour, they are by no means finely potted or finished, and suggest that the materials and methods were never really under perfect control. The body was of the artificial glassy type, though it varies within rather wide limits. Sometimes it was opaque, but it was often very rich in frit, and must consequently have been a difficult body to manage in practical working. The glaze is whiter than the early glazes of Chelsea and of Bow, probably because it was very slightly " blued " with cobalt, and it generally has a cold, glittering look, quite unlike that of the other china glazes of the period. The potting is clumsy, almost rude, and the forms of the vases, leaf basins, figures, and candlesticks are heavy and entirely lacking in grace or elegance. The most characteristic feature of the porcelain is, however, the underglaze blue colour already referred to, which is so different from that on any other English porcelain, that it frequently suffices to distinguish the pieces on which it occurs. This blue is lighter in tint than Chelsea, and brighter than any Worcester or Derby blue. It has a curious " run," streaky look, and often presents such an uneven appearance as might be expected

* *See* Bemrose, p. 18.

had it been applied on the biscuit ware with a piece of rag or sponge instead of a brush. The objects reproduced on Plate X. show not only the quality of the colour, but also two characteristic methods of using it. The little figure group of " Cupids and Goat " has been rudely ornamented with patches of colour coarsely applied. The other piece reproduced on this plate is evidently one of those " leaf basons " mentioned in the sale advertisement of 1757. Both the basin and cover are shaped as if they were formed of overlapping leaves. This seems to have been one of the stock devices of the factory, for it was used in plate borders as well as in vases and other objects. The blue colour is here used in a more definitely decorative way. It is no longer roughly spotted about the piece, but alternate leaves are coloured with it, so as to produce a radiating ground pattern of blue and white. On the white panels little groups of flowers are enamelled in colours ; but on the blue panels, ornamental cartouches are very delicately but finely outlined in raised white enamel. This finely-drawn rococo scrollwork in raised white enamel on a blue ground is again most distinctive of the productions of the factory. Another illustration of its use will be found on the rim of the plate in Fig. 29, which evidently belonged to one of the dessert services known to have been made at Longton Hall. Mr. Bemrose * gives an illustration of an interesting dish in the possession of Mr. T. Boynton, F.S.A., with vine leaves and grapes modelled in low relief and coloured with the streaky blue. This was probably one of the fruit dishes of such a dessert service.

Attention should be drawn to the sparing use of gold on the products of Longton Hall. When it does occur, it has all the appearance of thickly applied leaf-gold attached with japanner's size and afterwards stoved. It never seems to have been burnt into the glaze, and so cannot be regarded as a true form of pottery gilding at all.

Figures are not prominent among the productions of the factory. A few figures and groups are known, such as those in

* " Bow, Chelsea, and Derby Porcelain," p. 164.

FIG. 29.—PAINTED VASE WITH FIGURES.
PLATE WITH BLUE RIM, SHOWING
WHITE ENAMEL CARTOUCHES ON
THE BLUE.
LONGTON HALL.

the British Museum and in the possession of Mr. Bemrose and Mr. Boynton,* but they are neither very skilfully modelled nor very tastefully coloured. They are invariably placed on clumsily shaped rococo scroll-work bases, which have a few lines of enamel colour carelessly applied on the edges of the scrolls, but in a half-hearted, unsystematic manner.

The most elaborate ornamental pieces of the factory were un-doubtedly the vases and beakers, and these were generally squat and clumsy in shape, and often hideously disfigured by the rough rococo scroll-work (sometimes taking the form of rolls of clay applied to the sides of the pieces), and by the curious use of flowers modelled in the round and stuck upright on the rim. Of this type is the vase figured by Professor Church in his " English Porcelain." The vases in the Franks collection, one of which is shown in Fig. 29, though by no means models of elegance, are much better shaped and better made than these. The handles are heavy, but are well attached to the body of the vase, and the applied flowers are simple and well shaped. The most important feature of these vases is found, however, in the panels painted with groups of figures, evidently taken from engravings after Watteau, but drawn in such a way that, while they are decidedly French in style, they are also curiously reminiscent of similar work on some of the Chelsea vases of the later period.

Longton Hall pieces are seldom marked, but when a mark occurs it is generally in the form of two crossed " L's," which probably stand for Littler, Longton.

In the appendix of marks will be found examples photographed from pieces in the British Museum.

* It is interesting to note that the candlestick, figured in Mr. Bemrose's book, p. 163, occurs in a totally different garb as a Bow or Chelsea piece in the Schreiber collection. The figure of Winter also occurs. If the pieces described by Mr. Bemrose are genuine Longton Hall figures, then it is probable that the pieces in the Schreiber collection were made at Derby after the transfer of the Longton Hall moulds, etc.

G

CHAPTER IX.

DERBY.

THANKS to the researches of Jewitt and Bemrose, the establishment of the porcelain works at Derby, which played such an important part in the development of English porcelain, and which took over the moulds and models, as well as some of the traditions, of the factories of Chelsea, Bow, and Longton Hall, has now been fixed beyond doubt. Whatever tentative efforts may have been made in Derby as early as 1750, they can have had little influence on subsequent developments. The factory in Nottingham Road, which was to attain such prominence from 1770 to 1840, was begun in the early part of the year 1756, when William Duesbury converted a few cottages into workshops. This fact corresponds with the unsigned deed first mentioned by Jewitt, dated January 1st, 1756, by which John Heath, of Derby, in the county of Derby, gentleman ; Andrew Planché, of the same place, china maker ; and William Duesbury, of Longton, in the county of Stafford, " enameller," " became co-partners together as well in the art of making English china as also buying and selling of all sorts of wares belonging to ye art of making china." By this deed Heath was bound to pay into the concern the sum of £1,000 only, for which he was to receive one-third of the profits till the principal sum was paid back. Apparently Planché and Duesbury were to manage the works, Planché bringing to the venture his knowledge of bodies and glazes, and Duesbury his knowledge of enamelling or decorating. John Heath was a well-known personage in Derby, being a scrivener, moneylender, and banker in partnership with his brother Christopher. In connection with his own immediate business he seems to have financed several industrial undertakings, for he is known to have been interested in the earthenware works at Cockpit Hill, Derby, as early as 1750—probably in the same way that he was interested in the undertaking of 1756, with Duesbury and Planché. Whether Planché had been working in a small way as a china-maker in Derby, or had been making experiments at the Cockpit Hill works, is not known. Neither have we any information as to how he obtained his knowledge of china-making. Mr. Jewitt's suggestion that he travelled on the Continent and picked up his knowledge of the manufacture of china at Dresden only serves to show how uncritical some of that writer's statements can be. The Dresden factory was as difficult to get into as it was to get out of,* and it was the home of "true" porcelain—a substance never made at Derby. It is much more probable that Planché had worked at Chelsea or at Bow, or that, as he is stated to have been born in England of parents who were both French refugees, he may have learnt something from the French workmen who undoubtedly came over to Chelsea. But very little is really known about the man or his work; there is, indeed, no record of his connection with the Derby factory, save in this unstamped agreement, so that his exact position must remain uncertain.

The biography of William Duesbury is far less obscure. We know that he had worked in London as an "enameller," or decorator of pottery, and that he had risen to the position of an employer of enamellers, carrying out work for the principal London dealers.† In 1755 he was living at Longton, Staffordshire, and it has been suggested that he was concerned in the Longton Hall works. His whole career proves that he was a man of great energy and industry, for he developed in a comparatively short period into an excellent man of business, conducting what, for his day, must be considered extensive operations. We may suggest that, having made some money as a master enameller, he was ambitious to become a

---

* *See* p. 5.   † *See* p. 39.

manufacturer. With this intent, no doubt, he left London in 1754, and went down to Longton where his father lived, in the hope that he might readily obtain a partnership in the recently established Longton Hall factory. Finding the manufacturing processes in use there too experimental and uncertain, and making or renewing the acquaintance of Planché, who was living at Derby, (only some thirty miles away,*) he proposed that they should set up a new factory. They approached Mr. Heath—as two practical men having between them competent knowledge of the making and decorating of porcelain as it was carried on in London—and the partnership deed was drawn up and presumably carried into effect. Duesbury must have been the active spirit of the concern, and gradually got the business entirely into his own hands, for when the Heaths failed in 1780, and the Cockpit Hill pottery works had to be sold with all its stock, the Derby porcelain factory was not affected as it would have been had John Heath retained any interest in it. In 1770, when the Chelsea works was leased by Duesbury, Heath was still interested in the Derby factory, for the lease was granted to " William Desbury and John Heath, their executors, administrators, and assigns," † so that the partnership must have been terminated after that date. In 1775 or 1776, when the moulds and stock of the Bow works were purchased and removed to Derby, the only name mentioned in the transaction is that of William Duesbury. It was evidently Duesbury's ambition to become the principal porcelain manufacturer in England, and as the various early factories languished or died, Duesbury bought them. In the case of Longton Hall and Bow, he seems to have dismantled the works and removed such plant as he required to Derby ; but where, as in the case of Chelsea, the reputation of the factory was a valuable asset, he carried on the works separately for a number of years before finally closing it. The insignificant sum which was paid for the Chelsea works and stock has already

* It is not generally realised that Longton is little more than 30 miles by road from Derby.

† Note the erratic spellings of the name Duesbury, which occurs here as Desbury, and elsewhere as Duesberry, Dusberrie, and Duesbrie.

PLATE XI.

Two Derby Dessert Plates,

WITH BLUE BORDERS RICHLY GILT, AND PAINTED CENTRES.

Victoria and Albert Museum. From the Jermyn Street Collection.

(*See p.* 97.)

been mentioned,* and the Derby factory, even after the other factories had been closed and amalgamated with it, cannot have been a large one. Haslem, who worked at the factory in the early part of the nineteenth century, gives, in his book, " The Old Derby China Factory," good reason for believing that the works could not have found employment for more than 90 or 100 workpeople in the time of the elder Duesbury †; while Hutton, in his " History of Derby," says that 70 workpeople were employed there in 1790, when the old works was in a flourishing condition. The first William Duesbury died in 1786, and was succeeded by his son William, who carried on the business till 1795. In that year he took into partnership Mr. Michael Kean, a clever miniature painter, and the firm became Duesbury and Kean. The second William Duesbury, however, died in the following year (1796). Kean, who managed the business, shortly afterwards married his widow, and carried on the works for the joint benefit of himself, his wife, and Duesbury's family. Kean was a clever man and an artist of some ability, but, apparently owing to domestic differences, the partnership of Duesbury and Kean, into which by this time the third William Duesbury had entered, was dissolved about 1811, and Kean left the works. It may be mentioned that Kean had leased in his own name a piece of land adjoining the works, and had erected there an earthenware factory in 1797. This venture had a very short life, as it seems to have been abandoned in 1799. The two works communicated by a narrow passage, and Haslem states that, on the cessation of the earthenware undertaking, the porcelain-making business was removed into the new factory. This placed more rooms at the disposal of the proprietors, and during the period from 1811 to 1840 as many as 200 workpeople seem to have been employed when trade was good. The third William Duesbury (Kean's stepson) never seems to have taken any active share in the business, and he was only twenty-three years of age when, owing to the rupture with Kean, the partnership was terminated some time between 1809 and 1811. The

---

* *See* p. 52.   † *Opus cit.,* p. 34.

works was disposed of as a going concern to Mr. Robert Bloor, who had formerly been employed as clerk and salesman under the Duesbury-Kean management. He took over the business in 1811 under covenant to pay certain small annuities, and the sum of £5,000 in instalments. It is said that in order to pay off this purchase-money, Bloor decorated the large stock of defective pieces that had been accumulated during the better period of the factory, and sold them by auction in the various large towns of Great Britain and Ireland. He thus established a custom which certain small Staffordshire firms still continue ; and so-called Crown-Derby Japan patterns always find ready purchasers at such sales to this day. This plan of selling slightly decorated and hastily finished goods by auction, enabled Bloor to pay off his debt of £5,000, together with interest, by the end of 1822 ; but the custom encouraged the production of very inferior articles and thus contributed to the downfall of the works. It must not be forgotten, however, that the early part of the nineteenth century was a trying period for all artistic manufactures in England, and the decline of the productions may have been due quite as much to general as to special causes. The artistic decadence was certainly not confined to Derby, but was common to all the English pottery works alike. The most probable cause of the downfall of the Derby works will be found in the fact that Bloor became mentally deranged in 1828, and remained in that condition till his death in 1846. During this period the works was managed by Mr. John Thomason, and, however conscientious and upright he may have been, it is impossible that he can have conducted the business with the enterprise that its proprietor would have displayed. A Mr. Clarke, who had married Bloor's grand-daughter, took out a statute of lunacy in 1844, and carried on the works in a very diffident fashion till the end of 1848, when they were finally closed. In 1849 the whole of the plant, stock, moulds, and raw materials were purchased by Mr. Boyle, of Fenton, Staffordshire, and were removed to that place, only to be again disposed of, or broken up, within a few years.

It should be said that on the closing of the old works a small factory was started by some of the old Derby hands in King Street, with Mr. Locker, formerly Bloor's chief clerk, as managing partner. This works has continued to the present day, and is now carried on by Mr. Sampson Hancock, whose great-great-grandfather was an apprentice of the first William Duesbury.

In 1876 a new and distinct company was formed in Derby, with a works in Osmaston Road. This company is now known as the Royal Crown Derby Porcelain Co., but it has no direct connection with the historic Derby works, the history of which will alone be treated here.

It is obvious that the productions of a factory which had an uninterrupted history of nearly a century (1756–1848) must exhibit great variations not only in technical skill, but in design and decoration. The changes of taste through such a long period would account for much, but as, in addition, the four proprietors—the two Duesburys, Kean, and Bloor—differed widely in their training and ideas, the variations in the products of their works were greatly accentuated. The elder Duesbury had been educated as a china decorator, and seems to have been rather a shrewd business man, with a keen eye to the current public taste, than an artist of striking individuality. The second William Duesbury had been brought up to the business from his youth, and had doubtless received a much better education and training than his father; at all events, in his time the factory seems to have reached its highest limit of excellence in the production of elaborately painted pieces, and of the finely modelled statuettes and groups which belong to Derby alone, and were not made from Bow or Chelsea moulds. Kean was also an artist, and it was apparently through his influence that the style known as Derby-Japan was introduced. Bloor, on the other hand, had been only a salesman or clerk; he had had no training either as workman or artist such as would have enabled him to add to the reputation of the factory. Considering the man and the age in which he lived, it is not remarkable that his ownership of the works should coincide with its period of decline.

Singularly little is known concerning the doings of Derby before Duesbury acquired the Chelsea works in 1770 ; and yet during the fourteen years that had elapsed since he had begun business as a manufacturer considerable progress must have been made to warrant him in buying the factory at Chelsea. Evidently no mark was used on the early pieces, and it is almost certain that many pieces attributed to Bow and Chelsea were made at Derby. Mention has been made of a candlestick and a small figure of Winter in the Schreiber collection, the first being attributed to Bow and the second to Chelsea.* The well-known figures of the Derby dwarfs, and the Tythe-pig group, in the same collection should by their style of modelling and of enamelling be attributed to Derby and not to Chelsea. These few instances are probably typical of many others which will be found by future research. As early as December, 1756, an advertisement appeared in the *Public Advertiser*, " by order of the proprietor of the Derby Porcelain Manufactory," in which mention is made of " a curious collection of fine figures, jars, sauce-boats, services for desserts, and great variety of other useful and ornamental porcelain, after the finest Dresden models." Again, in May, 1757, notices appeared in the *Public Advertiser* of a sale of china, and the first item mentioned is " the largest variety of the Derby or second Dresden."

It is evident that the " gentle art of advertising " had made considerable progress by the middle of the eighteenth century, for it is impossible that anything worthy of such commendation can have been made at Derby at that date. It has been suggested that figures had been made at Derby long before 1756, and Mr. Bemrose has remarked that a few figures are specially mentioned as Derby, among those enamelled by Duesbury in 1751–3, when he was working in London ; but they are very few in number, and there is nothing to show that either they, or the Staffordshire figures mentioned in the same work-books, were porcelain at all. There may have been some manufacture of small and unimportant

* *See* p. 81 (footnote).

FIG. 30.—RODNEY JUG.
DERBY.

figures at the Cockpit Hill pottery works, but these would most likely be made in some form of earthenware. If so, the moulds were probably at Cockpit Hill, and as Heath the banker was interested in both factories, such moulds may have been transferred to the porcelain works at its commencement in order that the figures, whatever they were, might be made in the finer material. That small figures were produced in quantities during the early years of the factory is shown by the mention in an account of goods sent to London in 1763 of " Small rabbets (!) at 2s.," " chickens at 2s.," " bucks on pedestals at 2s. 6d.," " second-sized boys at 1s. 6d.," " large-sized pidgeons (!) at 7s.," "bird-catchers at 10s. 6d.," "small baskets at 2s. 6d.," "standing sheep," "feeding sheep," and "cats." In the same consignment mention is made of much more important statuettes and groups. " Large Brittanias " (!) " Shakespeare," " Milton," " large quarters " (of the Globe), " Jupiters," " Leda," " Europa," " Mars and Minerva," " Neptune," " the Muses " (which range in price from 12s. to 68s. each) ; and also of a variety of useful articles, such as " flower jars," " inkstands," " honeycomb jars," " Chelsea pattern candlesticks," " Dresden pattern candlesticks," " beakers," " polyanthus pots," " open-work baskets," " octagon fruit-plates," " fig-leaf sauce-boats," " vine-leaf plates," " coffee-pots," " butter tubs," and " teapots." There is no information as to the nature of the body and glaze of these early pieces, and many of the pieces that may with probability be attributed to this period are so covered with enamel colour that it is difficult to determine the exact nature of the porcelain itself. It is almost certain that the body was a glassy body of the same type as the early productions of Chelsea, Bow, and Longton Hall. By 1764, at least, experiments were being made to discover some different composition for the body of the ware, as Richard Holdship, who had been a partner in the Worcester factory, undertook for certain considerations " to impart in writing to Duesbury and Heath his secret process for making china according to the proofs already made by him, and to supply them with all sufficient quantities of soapy rock at fair prices."

This was evidently the soapstone used in the contemporary Worcester porcelain, but it is uncertain whether the process was ever carried into operation on the large scale. A change in the composition of the body apparently came in 1770. When Duesbury bought the Chelsea works, one of his first acts was to send ten bags of bone-ash to Derby, and he is hardly likely to have done that if bone-ash had been in use at Derby. The purchase of the Chelsea works with its receipts doubtless improved the knowledge of the Derby people, and probably it is from this time that we must date the use of bone-ash in the Derby body. Doubtless, the body would be made with bone-ash as well as with frit, from about 1770, down to the beginning of the nineteenth century, when the ordinary English body of china clay, china stone, and bone-ash was introduced.

In the account of the Derby-Chelsea ware, reference has already been made to the introduction of biscuit figures immediately after 1770. There is no mention of such pieces in connection with Sprimont's Chelsea porcelain, but in the first sale of the united output of the Derby and Chelsea factories, in April, 1771, they were given a prominent position. It is therefore almost certain that such pieces had been made at Derby before this date, and they certainly continued to be made down to a late period. The texture of the biscuit figures varies within rather wide limits, and the composition of the body for biscuit varied too.* Mention has already been made of some of these pieces, especially those in which the biscuit figures had pedestals or accessory supports coloured and gilded.† The finest figures, however, seem to have been made at a later period, probably between 1790 and 1810, when two or three clever modellers were employed at the works. The first of these was a Swiss named Spengler, who came to Derby in 1790,‡ and seems to have modelled many groups mainly taken from pictures by Angelica Kaufmann,

---

* That is, the special body which was not intended to be glazed.

† *See* p. 56.

‡ Mr. Bemrose publishes on pp. 126–129 of his work a copy of the agreement between Spengler and the second William Duesbury.

FIG. 33.—"THE DEAD BIRD" (BOY).
MODELLED BY SPENGLER.
DERBY.

FIG. 32.—"ZINGARA."
MODELLED BY SPENGLER.
DERBY.

FIG. 31.—"THE DEAD BIRD" (GIRL)
MODELLED BY SPENGLER.
DERBY.

whose pretty, quasi-classical compositions were then the height of fashion. Of this type are the two figures reproduced in Figs. 31 and 33, in which the attitude of the weeping girl with the birdcage, and of the youth digging the grave for the dead bird, are instinct with the spirit of trivial sentimentality that characterises so much of the minor art of the period. Numerous Cupid groups were modelled by Spengler from the same source : " nymphs awakening Cupid by tickling his ear with a straw," " three nymphs pelting with flowers a Cupid bound to a tree," and " a set of the elements represented by groups of Cupids," are the best known of these. The famous group of figures known as the " Russian Shepherds " is one of Spengler's most noteworthy efforts.

Greater spirit and artistic skill are shown in the portrait statuettes of British generals and admirals modelled at about the same period by Stephan. Of these the figures of Lords Rodney, Hood, and Howe are the best known. The figure of Lord Howe reproduced, in Fig. 34, from the specimen * in the British Museum, shows not only the skill with which the figure had been modelled, but also how perfectly fitted the old Derby biscuit was for such a purpose.

Another modeller, W. Coffee, was also employed for a few years after Stephan left the works. He seems to have modelled mainly rustic figures and animals. His most celebrated piece is a figure of a young shepherd with dog and sheep. He is said to have taken a cast of a figure of Adonis, and then disguised it by clothing, in order to produce this figure.

In the earlier pieces of the biscuit body, such as those of the Derby-Chelsea period (1770–1784), the material is not very highly vitrified, and some of the figures have a somewhat yellow tint, probably having in the hundred and thirty years or so of their existence become slightly stained. The pieces of the period from 1790 to 1810, or thereabouts, when

---

* These portrait statuettes appear to have been copied or adapted from engravings after contemporary portraits. The " Lord Howe " was probably produced in 1794 to commemorate the " Glorious 1st of June," when Howe gained his great victory over the French fleet off Ushant.

in the finest condition, show a "waxy" surface, having been so far vitrified that light penetrates some little distance into the material, producing a soft and pleasing effect, but there is little or no sheen, and every detail remains as crisp as when the figure left the hand of its maker. Sometimes the figures of this period do exhibit a decided sheen upon the surface that must be due to a slight coating of glaze, probably obtained by the process known as "smearing." In this process the biscuit piece is subsequently fired in the glazing oven in close proximity to richly glazed pieces, or to some volatile glazing compound, and thus receives an infinitely fine coating of glaze, such as cannot be obtained in any other way. Any good collection of Derby biscuit figures will exhibit all these varieties of surface among the pieces. Thus, in the British Museum collection the figures of George III. and of Catherine Macaulay are of the earlier type, the "Lord Howe" and the "Zingara" are the perfection of the best type, while the figures of the "Dead Bird" group exhibit the condition of glossy surface which is probably due to "smearing," and it must be said that their texture is in consequence less pleasing than that of the other pieces.

After the works passed into the hands of Bloor, the quality of the biscuit body deteriorated greatly. The material had always been a special composition rich in glassy frit, and the pieces had to be fired in the coolest part of the biscuit oven, or else they would have sunk quite out of shape. The difficulty of producing the special body under the changed conditions of the factory led to its disuse ; the later figures were made in the ordinary body employed for the other productions of the works, and so have a dull, heavy, and at the same time "chalky" look, that compares unfavourably with the earlier examples. It must be said, too, that the contrast between the ordinary glazed and enamelled figures and those in the biscuit body is astonishing. The biscuit figures are often both skilful and tasteful, but the coloured figures are frequently the reverse. The animals and figures already referred to are generally covered with sticky-

FIG. 34. – LORD HOWE.
BISCUIT PORCELAIN.
DERBY.

looking enamel colours, and are sometimes modelled in what is supposed to be a "grotesque" style, which gives a very poor impression of the taste of whoever was responsible for them. Figures with pet animals, shepherds and shepherdess with garlands and bouquets, dancing figures with musical instruments, laughing figures, grotesque seasons, and other figures such as one would expect to find in country cottages were produced in profusion during a great part of the life of the factory. Occasionally the enamelled figures of Chelsea were reproduced, and specimens of the well-known Falstaff, and of Garrick as Richard III., made at Derby are by no means rare. The production of fresh figure subjects continued down to the end of the old factory, but the modellers were not such workmen as those employed during the best period. They continued the practice of working from contemporary prints, so that we find at least a dozen figures and groups illustrative of "Doctor Syntax," together with such figures as "Grimaldi as Clown," "Liston as Paul Pry and Dominie Sampson," and "Madame Vestris in 'Buy a Broom.'" The well-known set of French figures, "The Paris Cries," was also copied at this later period, and figures of Napoleon, Nelson, and George IV., were produced, but in a style very inferior to the earlier statuettes of the famous admirals of the eighteenth century.

It is singular, considering the important part that the production of elaborate vases played at Chelsea, both under the direction of Sprimont and of Duesbury, that comparatively few vases appear to have been made at Derby itself during the eighteenth century. The Duesburys probably realised that the extensive manufacture of such elaborate and expensive pieces was not likely to add to the commercial success of the factory, and it was not until the nineteenth century that any large or notable pieces of this description appear to have been made. It cannot be said that these late vases add anything to the artistic reputation of the works. The most famous examples are "the Hutchinson vase," made in 1802, for Sir John Hely Hutchinson, who succeeded Abercromby as Commander-in-Chief in Egypt; and "the King's vases," made for presentation, on behalf of the workpeople of the factory, to William IV. after the passing of the Reform Bill of 1832. The Hutchinson vase was twelve inches high, shaped somewhat on the lines of an antique " Crater," but heavy and inelegant in its proportions. It was decorated with elaborate paintings ; on the front, the arms of the borough of Derby (a buck in a park) ; on the reverse, the Hutchinson arms, in proper colours. The King's vases were of the same shape with different handles, but were mounted on bases, and had covers surmounted with figures, made from old Chelsea models—one of Wisdom, the other of Justice. The ground colour was the famous Derby Mazarine blue, richly gilt ; and in the panels were views of Windsor Castle and the seats of the principal Ministers who had been instrumental in passing the Reform Bill. With stand and cover they were no less than 33 inches in height, and altogether they furnished a striking proof of the degradation of taste at this period.*

The well-known Rodney jug, made and decorated by the workmen for use at their benefit club meetings as early as 1782, is a model of taste and elegance in comparison with these vases. It is noteworthy, too, because it fixes for us the date of at least one characteristic style of the Derby factory. The jug was doubtless made to commemorate the victory of Lord Rodney over the French Admiral De Grasse, and is inscribed with the date of the battle—" April the 12th, 1782." The reproduction, in Fig. 30, is from a replica, now in the British Museum, of the historical piece which belonged to the " Rodney " Club. The spout of the jug is formed of a mask of Rodney, and the way in which the cocked hat has been touched into shape so as to furnish a spout that would pour well, is extremely skilful. The way in which the spout recalls the figure-head of a ship is also very striking. The large floral sprays painted on each side of the jug are attributed to Withers, one of the earliest Derby painters of whom we have any definite

* These vases were never presented to the King as intended, the responsible ministers considering that presents of this kind should not be accepted by the Sovereign. They were afterwards sold and the money subscribed was returned to the workpeople.

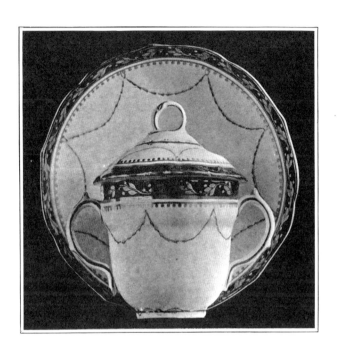

FIGS. 35, 36, AND 37.—TEA WARE, TYPICAL
DERBY PATTERNS.

DERBY.

knowledge. They are admirable examples of the formal, stereo-
typed style of flower painting common to all the porcelain factories
at this period.

"Useful" rather than "ornamental" wares formed the staple
productions of the Derby factory during a great part of its history,
though many of the table services and tea-sets were so lavishly
decorated that they were probably kept quite as much for show as
for use. A careful examination and comparison of existing pieces
serves to show that the shapes and decorations of the early period,
say before 1790, were simpler than those of the later periods. We
know from the sale lists and advertisements that the elder
Duesbury prided himself on his copies of Sèvres and Dresden
models,* and it was only natural in such circumstances that a
certain amount of elegance and refinement should be found in
some of the pieces. The three examples of tea ware reproduced
in Figs. 35–37 illustrate this point very clearly. The shapes
of the cups (Figs. 36 and 37) are not only refined and graceful,
but they are true pottery shapes, and show a sympathetic feeling
towards the material that is rather rare at Derby. The smaller
fluted cup shown in Fig. 35 is quite ordinary in comparison with
the other two, though it is much to be preferred to the commonest
Derby shapes, such as the mugs and "coffee cans," produced in
great profusion, which are absolutely clumsy and commonplace.
The decorative enrichments on these three pieces are also interesting.
The simple blue band (*see* Fig. 35), with little sprays of painted
flowers, formed one of the stock devices of the Derby pot-painters,
and they seem to have carried it to nearly every English factory.
The two-handled covered cup (Fig. 36) is elegantly decorated in
the Sèvres style. The wavy borders of laurel in gold on blue
bands, and the delicate festoons painted in pink, form an appropriate decoration for pieces of this class. Another example of a
good Derby pattern of the early period will be found in Fig. 20.
This piece bears the Derby-Chelsea mark, but it has every appearance of being a genuine Derby production of the period between 1770

* *See* p. 25.

and 1786.* It is rather astonishing to find what a large proportion of the pieces made after 1786 were decorated with painfully naturalistic drawings of flowers, landscapes, birds, and insects, when one finds early pieces so good as those illustrated in Figs. 35–37, and 20. Elaborate flower, fruit, and figure painting formed the most distinctive feature of the decoration in the period of the second William Duesbury (1786–1796), and no doubt the attention paid to the Derby factory by the noblemen whose seats were in the vicinity had something to do with the prevalence of this taste. Indeed, it was quite a common practice at this time for lords and ladies to have services painted from their own drawings, or even to do the painting themselves. Lord Lonsdale had twenty-four plates painted with views in Cumberland, from his own sketches ; and Lady Margaret Fordyce, Lady Plymouth, and Lady Aubrey are mentioned as painting services for their own use. A good idea of the pieces decorated at the factory may be obtained from the illustrations of richly painted plates (*see* Figs. 38 and 39, and Plate XI.). The elaborately decorated plate (Fig. 38), with a group of children and lambs painted by Askew, is evidently from one of the expensive dessert services of the time. The painting is of great technical excellence ; the enamel colours have all sunk into the fusible glaze, so that the effect is extremely soft and luscious. Askew seems to have been the best figure painter employed at Derby, and in addition to subjects like the one illustrated, he painted figure compositions after the works of contemporary artists. Plates painted with Cupids by Askew are also well known. It must be pointed out that in the case of pieces like the plate in question, only the centre would be painted by Askew; the ornamental border would be painted by another workman, and the gilding would be executed probably by a third. The simple fruit dish (Fig. 39) is painted with flowers by a painter, William Billingsley, who has attracted more notice than any other Derby workman. He was apprenticed at the works in 1774, and seems to have

* This piece bears the decoration that figured as No. 11 in the Derby pattern book.

FIG. 38.—RICH PLATE (CENTRE PAINTED
BY ASKEW).
DERBY.

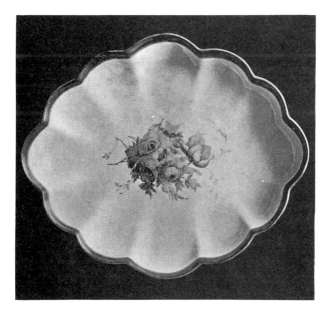

FIG. 39. – FRUIT DISH (CENTRE PAINTED
BY BILLINGSLEY).
DERBY.

succeeded Withers as principal flower painter about 1784, leaving the Derby works to commence his adventurous career as a china-maker in 1796. His doings will be referred to at some length in a subsequent chapter ; it will suffice to say here that he was a facile, clever workman, who painted groups of flowers, particularly roses, with great dexterity. Before his time, in flower painting on china the lights were left, as in water-colour drawing. Billingsley is said to have invented the not very painter-like device of washing-in the whole flower in colour and then wiping out the lights and modelling the flowers. Of course, he obtained a different effect in this way, but it is amusing to find what a reputation he gained by work that has no artistic distinction.

Examples of another style of dessert plate are given in Plate XI., where the painting of fruit and flowers in the centre plays a sub-sidiary part to the rich blue ground of the rim with its elaborate gilding. Such pieces are only interesting as examples of the careful and precise workmanship that was characteristic of the factory down to the end of the eighteenth century.

One of the most famous styles of Derby decoration remains to be mentioned—viz. the Crown-Derby Japan patterns devised in such variety during the first decade of the nineteenth century, and reproduced not only at Derby down to its close in 1848, but at almost every other English factory. These patterns were based on the famous Japanese designs known as Imari, and differed entirely from the earlier and simpler forms of Japan pattern used at Bow, Chelsea, or Worcester. Plate XII. gives a repre-sentation in colours of two Derby plates, a Derby saucer, and a contemporary Imari saucer. Since these patterns were introduced at Derby, they have been copied and vulgarised to such an extent that collectors generally have never paid them the attention they deserve. Pieces of this class are, of course, very strong and bright in effect, but their colour is generally harmonious and pleasing, and the patterns are arranged with a certain amount of real decorative skill, which is more than can be said for some of the pretentious modern styles. As will be seen from the illustrations in Plate XII., the colours

H

used were always a strong deep blue, a brilliant red inclining towards orange in thin washes, touches of green, and much flat gilding. At first the blue colour was painted under the glaze, but subsequently it was dusted on to the oiled surface of the fired glaze, and then fired again at the heat required to melt the glaze. In this way the glaze was stained through its substance, where the blue colour had been laid, and converted into a blue glass of great depth and richness. At this stage of the process, the piece would be simply covered with a kind of block pattern in dark blue and white. The red and green colours were then painted on the glaze, and the piece was gilded and received its final fire at a lower temperature in the enamelling kiln. The extent of the trade in these Japan patterns is shown by the fact that in 1817 Mr. Bloor had handbills circulated through the Staffordshire potteries, undertaking to find employment for " twenty good enamel painters who could paint different Japan patterns, borders, etc."

In the appendix will be found examples of many marks used at different periods on the wares of the Derby factory. The more important ones may be mentioned here. The earliest mark is said to have been a written " D," but this mark is exceedingly rare, and it is very doubtful if it was really used. The Derby-Chelsea marks already referred to (*see* p. 58) are the earliest that occur on any considerable number of pieces. Following these, and probably belonging only to Derby, is the " D " with a crown, which seems to have been used down to 1782, or thereabouts. It is generally found in blue, but it also occurs in green, in purple, and in rose colour. Shortly after 1782 the crossed batons and six spots were added to the crowned " D." This mark generally occurs in purple or puce, though it is also found in blue and in gold. A variation on this mark has the letter " K " combined with the " D," and this is supposed to distinguish the pieces made after 1795, when Kean was a partner. After the works passed into the hands of Bloor, his name was generally used on the pieces—" Bloor, Derby," with or without a crown. As these later marks were generally printed, they are more elaborate than the earlier ones. The

PLATE XII.

Imari Saucer.

Plate.

CROWN-DERBY JAPAN.

Plate.

CROWN-DERBY JAPAN.

Saucer.

CROWN-DERBY JAPAN.

Victoria and Albert Museum.

(*See pp.* 97-98.)

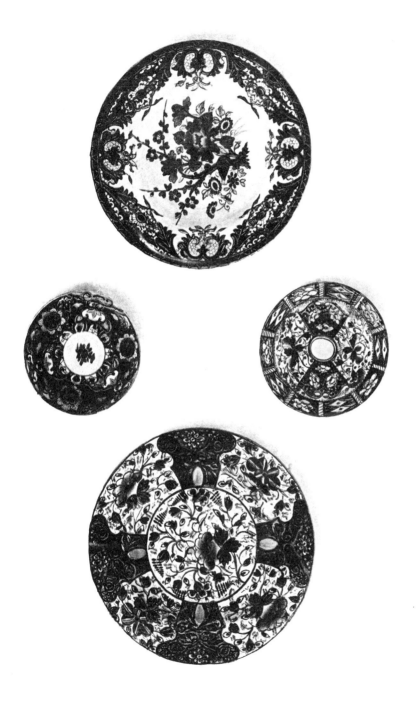

crown over a Gothic " D," printed in red, also belongs to the Bloor period. His marks are generally in red. The Crown-Derby mark with the batons and dots is sometimes found impressed in the bases or stands of figures produced after 1790. In addition to the regular marks, forged Dresden and Sèvres marks, generally painted in under-glaze blue, are found on no inconsiderable number of Derby pieces.

CHAPTER X.

WORCESTER.

AMONG the early English porcelain works, that at Worcester is the only one the origin of which has been clearly and definitely ascertained. The introduction of porcelain-making in that city has always been attributed to the labours of Dr. John Wall and William Davies, an apothecary, who were evidently carrying on experiments to this end in 1750, in a house in Broad Street, Worcester. The passion for making porcelain was just then at its height throughout Europe ; but these experiments of Wall and Davies might not have led to the establishment of the industry in Worcester, but for local political conditions. The people of the city and county of Worcester have always prided themselves on their steadfast loyalty, and at this time there was a strong and influential Jacobite party in the district. Feeling ran very high between this party and the supporters of the reigning dynasty, and elections were fought with the utmost bitterness. The Jacobite party generally managed to win the electoral contests, and the members of the other party were anxious to extend their influence, and to secure an accession of votes. The establishment of a porcelain manufactory would doubtless aid in this direction, and was, therefore, a project worthy of support. At all events, the principal shareholders of the company, formed by deed on June 4th, 1751, for carrying on " the Worcester Tonquin manufacture," were leading members of the Whig party in the city. In addition to Wall and Davies, there were thirteen other partners, the largest shareholders being Dr. W. Bayliss, Richard Holdship, and Edward Cave, well known as the founder of the *Gentleman's*

PLATE XIII.

Examples of Blues used at Worcester in the Eighteenth Century.

POWDER BLUE.

(*See p.* 110.)

MAZARINE BLUE.

(*See p.* 110.)

SCALE BLUE.

(*See p.* 110.)

ENAMEL BLUE.

(*See p.* 111.)

EARLY UNDERGLAZE BLUE PIECES.

Victoria and Albert Museum.

(*See p.* 103.)

Magazine. In this original deed * it is stated that Dr. Wall and W. Davies " possessed † the secret, art, mystery, and process of making porcelain," and, further, that R. Podmore and John Lyes had been already employed for some time by the inventors, and were to receive extra remuneration, " the better to engage their fidelity to keep such part of the secret as may be entrusted to them." Care was to be taken to protect the secret in other ways—no strangers were to be admitted to the factory, and even the keys of the outer and inner doors were not to be kept by the same person.

We do not know what was the exact share of either Dr. Wall or William Davies in the invention, but all the credit has been generally given to Dr. Wall, who, if all is true that is stated of him, must have been a very remarkable man. Thus, he is said to have been an excellent chemist (whatever that may have meant at this period), a physician in large practice, the author of several medical works of repute, and a chief supporter of the Worcestershire infirmary. Besides all this, he is described as an artist of ability, who, in addition to painting portraits and historical compositions, designed stained-glass windows at Hartlebury and Oriel College, Oxford. As all these statements are made by strong partisans, we may take the liberty of doubting if Wall were really such an admirable Crichton as has been supposed. Although the taste displayed in the early productions of Worcester is always attributed to his influence, there is no evidence to show that he took any active part in the management of the concern. He had wealthy and influential connections, and must have been of the greatest assistance in obtaining support for the venture. The actual manager of the works from the commencement was the William Davies already mentioned, and he continued in that position down to 1783—the end of the first period in its history.

The first home of the company was an old mansion known as

---

* The original deed was republished by Mr. R. W. Binns in 1883.

† It is singular that the word " possessed " should be used in this connection, and that there is no claim on the part of Wall or Davies to any actual discovery. It is possible, to say the least, that they had acquired the secret from some workman from one of the earlier English or Continental factories.

Warmstry House, situated on the left bank of the Severn, just below St. Andrew's Church. The works remained here until 1840, when they were removed to their present site, and Warmstry House is now absorbed into Dent's glove factory. Edward Cave, the proprietor of the *Gentleman's Magazine*, being one of the largest shareholders of the company, it is not surprising to find that a view of the works * and a notice of the new enterprise appeared in that publication in August, 1752. The announcement was also made that " A sale of this manufacture will begin at the Worcester music meeting † on September 20th, with great variety of ware, and, 'tis said, at a moderate price." This was probably the first extensive sale of the products of the factory, which seems to have been carried on in a quiet, leisurely way, and without any resort to the auction sales which have been already mentioned in connection with Chelsea, Bow, Longton Hall, and Derby. The circumstances under which the company was formed, if, as has been suggested, the venture was due almost as much to political as to commercial considerations, would probably account for this. With many wealthy Whig patrons to support them, the directors of the Worcester works could develop the industry in their own fashion, and had not, like other china makers of the day, to make only such articles as would please the popular taste.

The earliest known pieces, which are in white, appear to have been moulded from silversmiths' work, but they are of clumsy manufacture, and were possibly trial pieces, one of them bearing the inscription " 1751 " painted in blue under the foot. It is very doubtful if such pieces were ever produced in quantity, for the great proportion of the early pieces now in existence are cups, often without handles, saucers, mugs, and small plates decorated with paintings in underglaze blue. The excellence of Chinese blue and white porcelain must have appealed strongly to the directors

---

* Reproductions of this print will be found in Binns' " Century of Pottery in the City of Worcester " and in Jewitt's " Ceramic Art of Great Britain."

† This was the quaint title of the " Festival of the Three Choirs," which was instituted before 1723. The festival meeting of 1752 was held at Worcester, in the month of September.

PLATE XIV.

Worcester Sucrier.

FIRST PERIOD.

Worcester Sauce-boat.

FIRST PERIOD.

British Museum.

(*See pp.* 110-111.)

of the Worcester works, for at no other English factory was it so much imitated, and, it must also be said, nowhere else were such successful results obtained. The quality of the Worcester blue and white of this first period is remarkably fine, and with the plain shapes, the soft greyish blue colour, and the not too brilliant or transparent glaze, it remains unrivalled among the productions of English factories. The mug shown on Plate II., which is of fairly early date, will serve to indicate the distinctive style of this ware. The cylindrical shape has been thrown on the wheel, the walls are left rather thick, and the handle, formed from a thin roll of clay not moulded, is firmly attached. The decoration is obviously Chinese in character, and was doubtless a faithful copy of a Chinese original. Many forms of decoration were employed at Worcester, in which blue colour played an important part. A reference to Plate XIII. will show, in the two lower fragments, illustrations of the early blue and white specimens, and of the charming quality so often obtained. The three reproductions here mentioned are from pieces made within the first fifteen or twenty years, and it was during this period that all the best pieces with designs painted in blue were produced. Bowls, dishes, mugs, tea and coffee services, jugs and plates, seem to have formed the principal objects of manufacture ; and the elaborate vases, statuettes, candelabra, and other cabinet pieces, which figured so prominently among the productions of other English factories, were rarely made at Worcester. Gilding, again, was very sparingly employed in the decoration during this period. The earliest cups were usually made without handles, but after the first few years cups of larger size were made, and these generally had handles. Indeed, two-handled covered cups for caudle, broth, and chocolate were produced in large numbers during the first period. One of the common patterns on these larger cups was the embossed pine cone or imbricated pattern, which was also used at Bow, Chelsea, Derby, and Bristol. Illustrations of this pattern will be found in Figs. 18, 21, and 56, taken from Derby, Bow, and Bristol pieces.

This first period also saw the commencement of the manufacture of the cabbage leaf jugs, with a mask under the spout, and the sauce-boats, pickle dishes, and artichoke cups made in the form of leaves, as well as the curious rockwork and shell stands for sweetmeats that seem to have been so popular at all the eighteenth century factories. Mention must be made, too, of the open-work baskets, pierced dishes, and similar articles, very elegantly made, and, as a rule, simply decorated with patterns in underglaze blue. Two illustrations are given of early pieces of this class from the Worcester Museum. Fig. 40 is a beautifully made basket, with an applied flower at the interlacings of the basket work, slightly touched with blue colour ; this is in imitation of a well-known Dresden style. Fig. 41 is a dish with pierced border and raised shells at the angles ; here the pattern in underglaze blue plays a more important part, but both pieces are characteristic of the simple methods in use, and of the eminently satisfactory results obtained, in the period under review.

While it seems probable that the first pieces of printed porcelain may have been produced at Bow, or, at all events, on Bow porcelain printed at Battersea, the real development of printing, which has done so much to cheapen common porcelain, took place at Worcester. The first application of designs, printed from engraved copper-plates, in the decoration of pottery, has been variously claimed for the Worcester works, and for Sadler and Green at Liverpool. A careful examination of all the ascertained facts and references would, however, trace its origin to the use of printed patterns in the decoration of Battersea enamels.

Printing was in use at Battersea as early as 1752–53, according to contemporary accounts, and we have certainly no trace of such a method of decoration on pottery at that date. The earliest Worcester examples of printed ware can only be referred to the end of 1757,* and it seems most probable that Sadler and Green, of Liverpool, who thought of taking out a patent for

* In Bowcocke's note-books there is mention of printed Bow mugs and tea-cups as early as 1756.

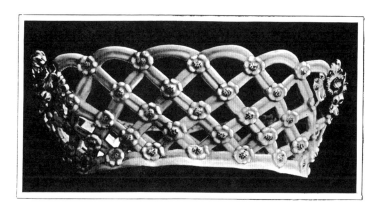

FIG. 40.—BASKET-WORK DISH :
     WORCESTER, FIRST PERIOD.

FIG. 41. — OVAL DISH, WITH PIERCED BORDER
    AND PATTERN IN UNDER GLAZE
    BLUE.
    WORCESTER, FIRST PERIOD.

their process about 1756, did not proceed with it, as they found that a similar process had already been used elsewhere. If this view be correct, the Battersea enamel works furnished the starting-point of the printing at Bow and at Worcester ; and Sadler and Green, of Liverpool, discovering the process independently, worked it for many years in the decoration of tiles and earthenware for the Liverpool and Staffordshire manufacturers.

At the Battersea enamel works the engraving of the copper-plates was in the hands of a skilful Frenchman named Ravenet, and one of his pupils was R. Hancock, whose fine delicate work has a very distinctive character of its own. One of his typical designs, known as " Hancock's Tea-party," occurs in various forms —as a small print on the enamelled back of a watch-case, in a larger size on pieces of Bow porcelain (one of which is illustrated in Fig. 28 from the specimen in the British Museum), and, with many similar patterns obviously due to the same hand, on a multitude of Worcester pieces. It would seem that Hancock worked at Battersea until the enamel works was abandoned owing to the failure of its proprietor, Sir S. T. Janssen, in 1756, and that he then migrated to Worcester, where he introduced the printing process. He was at Worcester in 1757, and the well-known mugs bearing the printed design of " The Apotheosis of Frederick the Great" were brought out at the end of that year, just after Frederick's great victory at Rossbach had made him the hero of the English public. Mugs and jugs bearing engraved portraits, evidently designed to meet the demands of the moment, or some sudden burst of popularity, seem to have been made in quantity. In addition to the Frederick mug we have others with portraits of the Marquis of Granby, the elder Pitt, King George II. with ships, emblems, and the inscription " Liberty," George III. and Queen Charlotte, and Roubiliac's statue of Shakespeare. No doubt the printing process was well adapted to the reproduction of such elaborate designs, and as any plain space of sufficient size could have a print transferred on to it, the same designs were used indiscriminately on mugs, jugs, punch-bowls, plates, and dishes, and, engraved to different sizes, on cups, saucers, tea and coffee pots, tea-caddies, mustard-pots, and all the varied productions of the works.

The credit of engraving this " Frederick " and many similar portraits has been claimed for Richard Holdship, one of the proprietors of the factory, but the suggestion is absolutely unfounded. There were two Holdships among the original proprietors ; this, Richard, is described in the partnership deed as a glover, and his younger brother Josiah as a maltster. Richard Holdship appears to have taken an active part in the business management during the first ten years or so, and it may have been at his instigation that the printing process was introduced, but it seems unfair to attribute any further share in it to him. Hancock's work was evidently appreciated, for he remained at Worcester as the principal engraver until 1774, and from 1772 he was one of the proprietors. His engravings were beautifully executed with a fine, precise, and delicate line, and, apart from any question as to the propriety of transferring engraved designs to porcelain, they remain among the finest specimens of such work that have ever been executed. The earliest engraved designs were printed in a jet-black enamel, and the general effect was somewhat like that of a line-drawing in sepia or Indian ink.* The process consisted in taking a print in the usual way from the engraved plate on to a sheet of thin paper. The piece of glazed porcelain was then heated and sized, so that the oily vehicle with which the colour was mixed would adhere to the glaze. The print was applied to the article and carefully but firmly rubbed. After standing a few minutes, the paper could be removed, and the print would be found transferred to the surface of the porcelain. Only the strongest colours would give an impression by such a process, hence the general use of black, of a purple which is often rather faint, and a bright red colour made from oxide of iron. The jet black and the red, when printed

---

* Some writers have most absurdly spoken of designs on porcelain in Indian ink, quite oblivious of the fact that had such a substance been used the fire would have burnt it away.

FIG. 42.—PRINTED SAUCER IN BLACK.
(SUBJECT : "L'AMOUR.")
WORCESTER, FIRST PERIOD.

from strong, freshly engraved plates, give very sharp impressions. The print of George III., in Fig. 44, is a remarkably fine example of Worcester printing in red, while the saucer (Fig. 42) is printed in black. This latter illustration is taken from a piece in the Victoria and Albert Museum, which possesses additional interest from the fact that it bears the inscription "RH. Worcester," which is supposed to be the signature of Hancock; while the anchor above has been ingeniously supposed to represent a rebus on the name of Holdship. There can be little doubt that the early printing was confined to work in enamel or on-glaze colours, for the plates used would not have carried sufficient depth of colour for satisfactory printing under the glaze. The pieces printed in underglaze blue, though of fairly early date, do not seem to have been made earlier than 1770, or thereabouts, and the frequent attribution of blue *printed* pieces to the first decade of the factory must be a mistake. The printed designs were, as usual, drawn from a variety of sources. Many of them were taken from contemporary engravings after great artists, such as Gainsborough and Watteau; while the books of designs by such men as Jean Pillement and Martin Engelbrecht, and the sporting prints of the day were also copied or adapted. Some of the engravings were, no doubt, designed by the engravers themselves, and the "Tea Party" (*see* Fig. 28), and "L'Amour"—a gallant kissing a lady's hand (Fig. 42)—which seem to have been favourite designs, are attributed to Hancock. Other engravers are also known to have worked at Worcester in the early period, of whom Ross and Valentine Green may be mentioned, but the work attributed to them is inferior to that of their master, Hancock.*

Some time after the introduction of printing, the process was, in the estimation of its producers, carried a step further by washing

---

* This remark only applies to Valentine Green's work for pottery. In 1760 he was articled to Robert Hancock, draughtsman and engraver to the Worcester Porcelain Company, for five years. At the end of this time he proceeded to London, and, adopting the profession of a mezzotint engraver, he produced some of the best English work in that style. He was elected an A.R.A., and was keeper of the Gallery of the British Institution in Pall Mall.

over parts of the printed design with flat washes of thin enamel colour. The result is very like that of a tinted engraving, and it forms a very unsatisfactory decoration for porcelain. In the description of Bow porcelain attention was drawn to the use of a similar process at that factory, but while the washes of enamel colour on the Bow pieces are very strong and the result is often gaudy and staring, the Worcester pieces are always thinly and delicately enamelled, and are not so much vulgar as merely tasteless. Although this kind of decoration was usually confined to plates, bowls, mugs, and tea-ware, it is occasionally found on more important pieces. The well-known large hexagonal vase in the Schreiber collection is of this class, and is a striking example of the absolutely inartistic results obtained by the mixture of printing and enamelling, where neither process has been really considered in relation to the other.

Down to about 1768 the production of table ware decorated with the simple underglaze blue painting, and with the enamel prints in black, purple, and red, seem to have contented the directors of the works, as we find very few pieces decorated with paintings in enamel colours after the manner so largely used at the London factories. This want of enterprise apparently provided an opening for some of the London enamellers to develop a business of their own in buying plain or slightly decorated Worcester pieces and enamelling them to suit the current taste. The following advertisement appeared in the *Public Advertiser* of January 28th, 1768 :—

"J. Giles,* China & Enamel Painter, Proprietor of the Worcester Porcelaine Warehouse, up one Pair of Stairs in Cockspur Street, facing the Lower End of the Haymarket, begs Leave to acquaint the Nobility, Gentry &c. that the said Warehouse is daily opened with a great Variety of Articles of the said Manufactory, useful & ornamental, curiously painted in the Dresden, Chelsea, and Chinese Tastes, superior to anything before exhibited to the Public on that Porcelain.

"As the enamelling Branch is performed in London by the said J. Giles,

* The Craft bowl so often referred to in the account of the Bow factory was fired in the kilns belonging to this J. Giles, or Gyles, in Kentish Town.

Fig. 43. — PRINTED PLAQUE FROM LINE
ENGRAVING.   PRINTED IN RED
ON GLAZE (CIRCA 1760).
WORCESTER.

Fig. 44. — SPECIMEN OF
BAT-PRINTING.
WORCESTER.

and under his Inspection, this Warehouse will be daily supplied with a Variety of new Goods, which will be sold as cheap as at the Manufactory, or any Place in Town, with the usual Discount to the Trade. As the Proprietor has a great Variety of white Goods by him, Ladies & Gentlemen may depend upon having their Commands executed immediately, and painted to any pattern they shall chuse."

Evidently J. Giles conducted his business on a wholesale scale, and his advertisement helps to account for the existence of many pieces of Worcester porcelain, enamelled in a fashion and with colours that one never associates with the genuine productions of the factory itself. Apparently in describing himself as " Proprietor of the Worcester Porcelaine Warehouse," Giles was assuming a position to which he was not entitled, for in subsequent insertions of the advertisement this title was omitted. The advertisement seems to have stirred up the Worcester people, however, as they shortly afterwards announced sales of their goods at the Exhibition Rooms, Spring Gardens, Charing Cross. In their advertisement it is stated that " some of their ware is advertised at another room, painted in London," but they go on to say that " the Worcester proprietors have engaged the best painters from Chelsea, and that they can execute orders in the highest taste and much cheaper than can be afforded by any Painters in London." This advertisement is of the utmost interest, as it not only proves that enamelling was being carried on at Worcester in 1768, but it explicitly states that artists from Chelsea had been engaged for this purpose. In the account of the Chelsea factory it was said that, owing to Sprimont's illness, little fresh work appears to have been done there after 1764. Mr. Binns was of opinion that the Chelsea artists migrated to Worcester about that year, but, if so, it is singular that we should have no earlier notice of their work than this advertisement of April and May, 1768.

With the advent of Chelsea painters new developments took place at Worcester. Larger and more elaborate pieces were produced, and even the ordinary table ware received quite a new style of decoration. Underglaze blue continued to be used, but mainly in the forms known as scale-blue and powder-blue. (*See* Plate XIII.) In these cases the ornament itself was no longer painted in blue, but that colour formed the groundwork of the piece, and white panels were reserved, or vignetted, to receive elaborate paintings of plants, exotic birds, fruit and flowers, in brilliant enamel colours. However apparent the Chelsea influence may be in the style and technique of these paintings, it is only fair to point out that the pieces, as a whole, have a character of their own— the character that one knows as " Old Worcester." Thus, both the scale-blue and powder-blue grounds of Worcester are quite distinct in tone and quality from the Mazarine or *gros-bleu* grounds of Chelsea. Examples of the use of these colours on tea-ware are numerous, but occasionally one sees large and important dishes and vases, in which the scale-blue ground and painted panels are shown to their full perfection. Plate XV. gives a representation of a fine dish of this class from the British Museum, while the large vases with birds in the Schreiber bequest are known to every collector. On the same plate another of the patterns that came into existence during this period is also illustrated. The " radiating trellis and vine " design is rather cleverly schemed, and must have been extensively used on tea services as well as on dessert plates and dishes. Modifications of it are shown on the plate (Fig. 50), where the trellis is used in combination with little sprays of flowers, and also in a teacup on Plate XIII., where it is used with lighter foliage dependent from a blue band enriched with gilding. The result in every case is a pretty and dainty style eminently adapted to its purpose.

It was only to be expected that the Chelsea painters should also bring with them to Worcester some of the rich enamel ground colours that had been invented at Chelsea. We get the apple or pea-green ground, a bright canary yellow ground (very seldom found at Chelsea), French green, sea-green, turquoise (pale), and a purplish crimson ground, evidently in imitation of the famous Chelsea claret colour. It is known from the advertisements that these colours were introduced as early as 1769, and the sauce-boat

PLATE XV.

Worcester Plate.

First Period.

Radiating Pattern of Trellis and Vine with Enamel Blue.

(*See pp.* 110-111.)

Worcester Dish.

Scale Blue Ground, and Exotic Bird Paintings.

British Museum.

(*See p.* 110.)

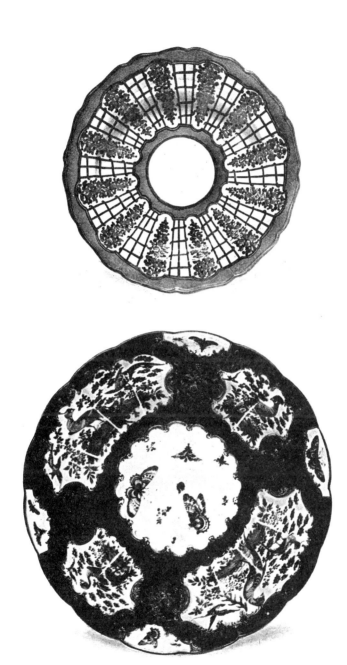

with yellow ground shown in Plate XIV., is believed to have been made in 1770.*

The slightly fluted shapes that had been produced at Worcester, almost from the commencement, lent themselves especially well to designs composed of delicately painted sprays with slight gilding. The tea-poy, on Plate XVI., is one charming example, out of many, of a characteristic style of the period, and is in itself sufficient to explain the fondness of our great grandmothers for the tea-ware of old Worcester. The covered sugar-basin (Plate XIV.) shows yet another style of decoration used for table pieces. With its pretty colour scheme and careful painting it has a character of its own quite apart from that of the Sèvres original which inspired it.

An enamel blue colour invented at Worcester † during this period is of singular quality. It is easy enough to get a bright blue under the glaze, but the early enamel blues, such as those of Bow and Chelsea, are often grey, even slaty, in tone. The blue in question is bright and intense ; sometimes it has a glossy, almost waxy, surface, but often it is quite dry. It generally occurs on tea ware, and is almost invariably used as bands, or as stripes, on broadly fluted pieces. An illustration of the colour and the general method of using it is given in the fluted teacup in Plate XIII., and in the plate border shown on Plate XV.

Another very characteristic Worcester style remains to be mentioned. This is the production of tea services in which the ornament, consisting generally of delicately drawn sprays of wild rose with leaves, buds, and flowers, is embossed in the paste. A sugar-bowl of this kind is reproduced in Fig. 46, but with insufficient justice to the delicacy of the original. If a piece of this kind is closely examined in a good light, the difference in thickness between the ornament and the ground gives such a difference in translucence that the pattern is most softly and gracefully relieved against the background. Indeed, it is not too much to say that pieces of this

---

* Two of these sauce-boats are in the British Museum collection.

† A Derby colour in imitation of this occurs on a plate border on Plate XI.

kind compare quite worthily with good Chinese pieces of modelled white paste. Mr. Binns states that these pieces were first made about 1780,* but judging by the quality of the paste, it seems probable that some of them are of an earlier date.

Stress has been laid on the fact that useful, as opposed to merely ornamental, pieces were produced during the first period. As a proof of this it may be pointed out that in the catalogue of the London auction sale of December, 1769, which lasted for five days, only four or five sets of covered jars and beakers are mentioned, and one set only can have been of any size or importance—viz. " A set of three elegant hexagon jars and covers of the very rich Mazarine blue and gold, beautifully enamelled in birds and insects," which sold for £8 15s.† Elaborately painted vases, beakers, and jars were certainly made from about 1768 to 1783, though apparently in no great quantity. On these pieces figure subjects, fruit, flowers, and landscapes, as well as the exotic birds so often mentioned, were painted with considerable skill. The work of Donaldson, who is supposed to have been a Chelsea artist, is held in very high repute, and the most famous examples of his painting are the three pieces —a vase and two beakers—in the possession of Lord Rothschild. The vase is 18¼ inches high, and the two beakers 12¼ inches. The ground is of rich blue colour, and the white panels left for the paintings are, as usual, enriched with rococo scroll borders in gold. The painted figure subjects, which are obviously after designs by Boucher, are " The Birth of Bacchus " on the large vase, and on the beakers the stories of " Leda " and " Europa." The style of the painting strongly recalls that on the late Chelsea vases, but the shapes are entirely different. The work of another painter, O'Neale, is also well known. He seems to have excelled in the painting of animal subjects, and in the famous collection of Mr. Dyson Perrins there are three vases with paintings representing lion, bear, and boar hunting scenes, evidently copied from Flemish

---

* Binns' " Century of Potting in the City of Worcester," p. 138.

† A similar set would probably sell for little less than £400 at the present time.

PLATE XVI.

Worcester Tea-poy.

FIRST PERIOD.

Schreiber Collection: Victoria and Albert Museum.

(See p. 111.)

engravings or paintings, which have his signature. A similar set of vases, signed by O'Neale, is said to have been in the possession of George Washington. Two of these pieces were exhibited at the Philadelphia Exhibition of 1876 among the Washington relics, and they bore O'Neale's name. A tea-set is known in which a different animal is painted on each piece, and these were probably executed by the same artist. A third artist, whose work is highly esteemed by collectors, was C. C. Fogo, who painted landscapes and scenes with figures, often in the Chinese manner.

The Chelsea influence was shown in yet another direction on elaborate Worcester pieces of this period. Vases, coffee-pots, beakers, and teapots are occasionally found in which the white panels bear paintings after Watteau's designs, exactly resembling those shown in the Chelsea tea service (Plate VIII.). There is no record of the artists by whom these pieces and the bird decorated wares were painted, but three Chelsea painters, Dyer, Mills, and Willman, named by Mr. Binns, were doubtless responsible for much of ' the work of this kind. These three men appear to have remained at Worcester into the early years of the nineteenth century.

The end of this first and finest period of old Worcester came with the sale of the works to Thomas Flight in 1783, but before entering on a description of his productions we must summarise the later history of the original company. Several of the first proprietors had died ; Richard Holdship sold his share in 1759, and was declared a bankrupt in 1760, and the company was reorganised in 1772 with a smaller number of proprietors, of whom Dr. Wall, the Rev. Thomas Vernon, William Davies and his son, and Robert Hancock, the engraver, were the chief. Owing to some dispute, Hancock was bought out for the sum of £900 in the year 1774, when he left the concern. Dr. Wall died at Bath in 1776, and as most of the other proprietors were advanced in years the business was disposed of, as just stated, to Thomas Flight, who had for some years previously been the company's London agent. He paid the sum of £3,000 for the business as a going concern, which does not

I

seem an extravagant sum, for the business had always been conducted on sound and reasonable, if somewhat unenterprising, lines.

Mr. Thomas Flight seems to have remained in London, and his sons, Joseph and John, who are believed to have been jewellers, came to Worcester to manage the works. An advertisement in the *Worcester Journal* in 1786 described Joseph Flight as "jeweller and china manufacturer," and this conjunction throws some light on the productions of the works during his management. As the Flights possessed no knowledge of the technical side of the business, they probably made as few changes as possible in the methods and processes of the factory. Almost immediately on taking possession they lost the services of Robert Chamberlain, who was the first apprentice of the original company, and who had risen apparently to the position of foreman decorator. Robert Chamberlain, with his son Humphrey, who was an indifferent artist, commenced to decorate porcelain at a small works in King Street, Worcester. As they were opponents of the existing factory they had to obtain their porcelain from elsewhere, and for some time they were supplied with pieces similar in shape to the old Worcester pieces, by Turner of Caughley. They seem to have received financial assistance from Mr. Richard Nash, of Worcester, and in 1788–89 they commenced the works at Diglis, Worcester, which, now greatly enlarged and improved, is still carried on by the Worcester Royal Porcelain Company. From this date, then, there were two factories in Worcester—the original works owned and managed by the Flights, and the works owned and managed by the Chamberlains. How strong the rivalry and how bitter the feeling between these two firms was, can only be realised by those who have been engaged in works similarly situated. The patronage of royalty and the nobility was sought with the utmost eagerness, and if some distinguished visitor could be secured for one factory, it was a matter for rejoicing to the favoured firm and for jealous disappointment to their trade rivals. Such facts as are needed to complete the outlines of our history may be summarised in the briefest manner.

FIG. 45.—SMALL SUGAR BOWL,
EMBOSSED ORNAMENT.
WORCESTER, FIRST PERIOD.

FIG. 46.—SMALL CUP AND SAUCER
POWDER-BLUE GROUND.
WORCESTER, FIRST PERIOD.

FIG. 47.—CUP AND SAUCER
(SECOND PERIOD)
WORCESTER.

FIG. 48.—TWO-HANDLED CUP AND SAUCER
(SECOND PERIOD).
WORCESTER.

THE OLD WORKS.

THE NEW WORKS.

1783. Joseph and John Flight acquire the business.

1788. Visit of George III. Use of the crown as a mark dates from this time.

1791. John Flight died.

1793. Joseph Flight took Martin Barr into partnership, Barr managing the works and Flight the London business. Flight and Barr period commences.

1807. Martin Barr, Junr., admitted to the firm, which became Barr, Flight, and Barr.

1784. Robert Chamberlain commenced to decorate porcelain.

1789. Robert Chamberlain and his son Humphrey, financed by Mr. Nash, built a new works—the nucleus of the existing Worcester works.

1827. Mr. John Lilly taken into partnership.

1828. The firm consisted of Walter Chamberlain (son of Humphrey) and J. Lilly.

1829. James Flight died. The business was carried on by the Barrs.

1840. The businesses of " Flight and Barr " and " Chamberlains " were amalgamated, and the production of porcelain was removed to the newer works (Chamberlains'), a tile business being carried on in the original Warmstry House works.

1847. Another rearrangement of the joint firm—the partnership between Barr and Chamberlain was dissolved and the business almost came to a standstill.

1850. Mr. F. Lilly and Mr. Kerr became partners in carrying on what business remained at the newer works (Chamberlains').

1852. Mr. Kerr was joined by Mr. R. W. Binns.

1862. The business was converted into a joint stock company, the Worcester Royal Porcelain Company, which continues to the present day.

A third factory needs passing mention. Just as Chamberlains' had split off from the original concern, this third firm established in 1800 by Thomas Grainger, a nephew of Humphrey Chamberlain, resulted from dissensions in the Chamberlains' business. The new firm was successively known as Grainger and Wood, and then, after 1812, as Grainger, Lee and Co. In 1839 George Grainger succeeded his father, and the business was carried on in his name down to 1888, when it was absorbed by the Royal Porcelain Company, who carry on the works in addition to their large factory.

The productions of the two leading factories must be considered separately, especially as there are well-marked differences of style and treatment between them. During the period when the Flights carried on the business of the original house (1783–1793) they went on reproducing as far as they could the things that had built up the fame of the business. Tea ware and table services again appear to have formed the staple business, as we hear very little of elaborate vases, beakers, or cabinet pieces generally. The first observable change is a growing precision and hardness, both in the shapes and decorations. The old simple blue and white pieces were gradually replaced by others designed and decorated after the fashion of Sèvres and Dresden. The two cups and saucers shown in Figs. 45 and 47 are good examples of the style of pieces made during the Flight period, and can readily be compared with the earlier pieces (Figs. 46 and 48) shown on the same page. No doubt to a certain extent this change commenced with the employment of the Chelsea artists, but down to 1783 the craftsmanship was free and often masterly ; after that date it gradually became more mechanical. This repetition of old designs at Worcester, as at

Fig. 49.—PLATE WITH BORDER
IN SCALE PATTERN.
WORCESTER.

Fig. 50.—PLATE WITH
"TRELLIS" BORDER.
WORCESTER.

other factories, often makes it difficult to fix the date of individual examples. The difficulty is perhaps not so great at Worcester as elsewhere, because the training of the Flights as jewellers seems to have given them a feeling for neat and precise workmanship, and this sometimes serves as a trustworthy indication of date, apart altogether from certain peculiarities of body and glaze to be mentioned presently. The two plates shown in Figs. 49 and 50 serve to illustrate this point. They are unmarked, and by the general style of their decoration they might be referred to the early period ; but an examination of the pieces themselves seems to prove that they are of later date, for the painting is altogether "tighter" than it would be on early pieces, and the colours are not so rich and strong. The shape of the plates, too, is somewhat more elaborate, and though not inelegant in itself, marks the commencement of the transition to the heavy and uninteresting forms of plates, with heavy gadrooned edges, so largely used between 1790 and 1850.

The production of richly painted and lavishly gilt dessert services seems to have been greatly encouraged by the visit of King George III. and Queen Charlotte to the works in 1788. In addition to purchasing elaborate services, the King bestowed on Messrs. Flight the privilege of styling themselves "China Manufacturers to their Majesties," and from that date the works was known as "The Royal Porcelain Works." The royal patronage thus bestowed on the factory was continued for many years, and was doubtless instrumental in obtaining for it the liberal support of the nobility and gentry. Unfortunately, this only meant, for the most part, encouragement of the needlessly elaborate, even extravagant services, in which taste and feeling were sacrificed to the most lavish display of gilding, with paintings of fruit, flowers, and birds in little panels, or with a huge coat-of-arms emblazoned in proper colours in the centre of the piece.* These "dress ser-

* No example is given of these services, but Fig. 69 reproduces a plate of a Coalport service decorated on exactly similar lines to these Worcester services.

vices " seem to have been commissioned by most of the noble families of the country, and continued to be made till 1851 or after. It would be difficult to imagine anything more tasteless than such services ; though the mere craftsmanship displayed in them is often admirable enough, they are only interesting as historical documents, which mark, in the most pronounced way, the degradation of taste that had come over not only the china factories, but the country at large. On Plate XVII. will be found a reproduction in colours of a plate of the Flight and Barr period, which will show that this criticism is not one whit too severe.

Mention must be made here of the introduction of another style of printing at the Worcester works, probably before 1790. In the earlier printing, the print was taken from a copper-plate engraved or etched with a line design, and was transferred to the porcelain from a sheet of paper. In this new process, known as " bat-printing," the engravings, which were generally of small size, were entirely executed in stipple. The engraved plate was covered with a thin layer of linseed oil, and then cleaned off with the palm of the hand until the oil remained only in the stippled dots. A thin cake, or " bat," of soft glue was pressed gently on to the plate, carefully removed, and at once applied to the glazed surface, so that the oil was transferred from the engraving to the porcelain. Enamel colour was carefully dusted over the piece, and, adhering only to the spots of oil, reproduced the design in colour, which was fused to the surface of the glaze by a subsequent firing. An illustration of this style of engraving (Fig. 43) appears side by side with a fine engraving of George III. in the older style. The process was, of course, only an ingenious application to porcelain of the stipple engraving so much in vogue at the period ; and the popular designs of Angelica Kaufmann, Cosway, and Bartolozzi were reproduced in profusion by this method not only on the tea-ware, but also on the plates and vases of the old Worcester factory down almost to its close.

The pieces manufactured by the rival firm of Chamberlains were

PLATE XVII.

Plate of the Service made for
Princess Charlotte

BY MESSRS. CHAMBERLAIN'S IN 1816.

Worcester Museum.

(*See p. 119.*)

Plate with Rich Gilding.

MADE BY FLIGHT AND BARR.

1793–1807.

naturally very similar in style to those of the parent factory, but they were generally less elaborate in their gilding and more slightly painted. There seems little doubt that at first they endeavoured to make a trade by offering the same style of pattern at a lower price. Before the end of the eighteenth century, however, they had commenced the production of "dress services," and there was the greatest competition between the two works as to which of them should secure these orders. Among the services of this kind made by the Chamberlains we must notice, for their historic interest only, a tea service made for Nelson in 1802, a breakfast service for the Duke of Cumberland in 1806, and an extraordinary service made for the Prince of Wales, in which every piece was of a different pattern. In 1816 a dessert service and a dinner service were made for the Princess Charlotte. We give a reproduction in colours of one of the dinner plates of this service (Plate XVII.), which, occurring on the same page as a rich Flight and Barr plate, will serve to illustrate the differences found in the work of the two factories.

We have already referred to the Crown-Derby Japan patterns, and the Chamberlains produced a great variety of patterns in the same style during the first thirty or forty years of the nineteenth century. It cannot, however, be said that the Worcester Japan patterns were equal to those of Derby. The blue colour is duller and heavier, and the workmanship of the red tracing and the gilding is more mechanical and stiff. The Worcester patterns are generally laboured copies of the Japanese originals rather than adaptations, as the best Derby patterns were. To add to the incongruity, it was a common device to run a deep border of Japan pattern all round a plate, and then to paint an English coat-of-arms in the centre with all the mechanical dexterity on which the Worcester heraldic painters prided themselves.

A short account must be given of the various bodies and glazes used at the Worcester works during the century from 1751 to 1851, which this history covers. The first body and glaze were undoubtedly very similar to those of all the early English factories—

namely, a fritted body very rich in glass, and a luscious soft glaze rich in lead. As we have seen, such body mixtures proved so difficult to work that attempts were very soon made at all the factories to discover others that would be more certain and more manageable. The experiments to this end seem to have taken a different direction at Worcester from elsewhere. The mineral steatite, or soapstone, which is an impure silicate of magnesia, was used in place of clay (silicate of alumina) to give a certain amount of plasticity to the ware. This substance rendered the body hard and infusible, and at the same time less transparent than the fine glassy porcelains. The glaze on this soapstone body was not a very fusible one, as it contained a certain proportion of ground Oriental porcelain, and some oxide of tin, which served to make it very " still," and slightly opalescent. The particularly fine, Chinese-like quality of the best Worcester blue and white is due to the composition of this body and glaze. When the soapstone was first used we are unable to say, but we shall learn in a subsequent chapter that it was being used in Bristol as early as 1750,* so that it may have been used at Worcester almost from the commencement of the factory. It must have been in use before 1760, as Richard Holdship, who severed his connection with the factory in 1759, apparently sold the receipt to Duesbury, of Derby, in 1764, and undertook to ensure a supply of soapy rock at reasonable prices. It is also uncertain how long the manufacture of the body composed mainly of glass and soapstone continued, but it is known that the Worcester company leased a Cornish mine of this mineral for 21 years, from 1770, and that they bought a 17 years' interest in the lease of another mine, held by Christian, of Liverpool, in 1776, for the sum of £500,† so that probably the soapstone body continued to be made largely, if not exclusively, at the old factory till toward the close of the eighteenth century. It is possible that bone-ash was used in small quantities at Worcester even as early as 1760, but it is very unlikely that it was extensively used until the

* *See* p. 130.
† *See* p. 157, also Binns' " Century of Potting, etc.," pp. 72, 115, 116

modern English body of bone-ash, china stone, and china clay was introduced, nearly a century ago. Mr. Barr spent much time in experiments for altering the Worcester body between 1800 and 1810, and in the year 1810 he stated that he had made " great improvements in the texture, whiteness, and beauty of our porcelain," so that it was probably about this date that the final change in the Worcester body was made. About 1818 the Chamberlains perfected and used for their most expensive services a body called the " Regent " body, which was apparently a glassy porcelain of the ordinary type, but it was so costly to manufacture that it was never brought into common use.

The marks on Worcester ware varied greatly in the early days of the factory. Many illustrations of typical marks of all the periods will be found in the appendix. It will suffice to say here that the earliest marks appear to have been the letter " W " (in script), which may have stood for Wall or Worcester ; and the crescent marks, which are found in simple outline, in solid colour, and in outline with shading lines. These marks, which occur of different sizes, are almost always in underglaze blue. A few instances are known of the crescent mark in on-the-glaze red, and in gold. Other early marks are imitations of Chinese seal marks, and curious scribble marks in which disguised letters and numerals are made to imitate Chinese signs. These invariably occur in blue, as do also the imitative Dresden marks, which, however, may often be distinguished by the occurrence of the numerals 9 and 91 between the points of the crossed swords. In addition to these regular factory marks, many workmen's marks are given by Binns and Chaffers.

The early printed pieces generally bear none of the usual factory marks, but many of them have the inscription " RH Worcester " finely engraved among the ornamental scrolls or groundwork (*see* Fig. 42). This mark is generally accompanied by an anchor.*
" R. Hancock fecit " also occurs on some of the early black printed pieces.

The later periods—1783–1793, 1793–1807, 1807–1813, and

* *See* p. 107.

1813–1840 are distinguished by the names or initials of the partners, impressed in the paste, painted in blue underglaze, and painted or printed in red overglaze. We thus have " FLIGHTS," or " FLIGHT "; " FLIGHT & BARR "; " FLIGHT, BARR, & BARR "; " BARR, FLIGHT, & BARR "; " F.B.B."; and " B.F.B." The first of these is sometimes associated with a crescent, and often, after 1788, the date of the visit of George III., the mark is surmounted by a crown.

The Chamberlain productions were generally marked with the word " Chamberlain's," in script, or with " Chamberlain's, Worcester," with or without the address of their London agency. Many of the later Chamberlain marks were printed.

CHAPTER XI.

PLYMOUTH.

THE porcelain factory at Plymouth only appears to have been in active operation for about three years (1768–1770), and the known pieces seldom show any remarkable degree of technical or artistic excellence. It has, however, the greatest interest for all students of English porcelain, as it represents the first successful attempt to produce "true" porcelain in England; and the materials used were entirely obtained from the county of Cornwall. Really the Plymouth works marks the fruition of twenty years of patient labour and assiduous research by a remarkable man—William Cookworthy, a chemist and druggist of that town. As early as the year 1745 Cookworthy, in writing to a friend, mentions the materials used by the Chinese in the manufacture of porcelain, and it is probable that from that time onward he never lost interest in the subject. As early as the year 1755 he is supposed to have found that the white clay which occurred so plentifully on the Cornish moorlands was very similar to the kaolin of the Chinese. We have already stated, however, that the discovery of kaolin was of very little use apart from a knowledge of the petuntse which was to be used with it. Cookworthy was fully acquainted with the accounts of Chinese materials and processes, sent to France by the Jesuit missionaries, and he therefore knew that two materials were required, and that one of them was a hard stone with green spots, which would melt in the fire. He discovered that the mineral known in West Cornwall as " growan," or " moor stone," would melt in the fire to a beautifully white mass, and he further found that certain specimens which showed abundance of green spots, melted most easily, so that he had little difficulty in identifying this material with the petuntse he was in search of. The date of this discovery is uncertain, but apparently Cookworthy knew of these materials for some years before 1768, and had been making laboratory experiments with them, heating them separately and in conjunction in crucibles, observing the effects of insufficient heat, of smoke, and of accidental impurities—all of which was doubtless of the greatest scientific interest to him, but went only a little way toward the establishment of a practical manufacture of porcelain. With the financial support of Thomas Pitt, of Boconnoc (created Lord Camelford in 1784), he commenced the manufacture in a small works at Coxside, " at the extreme angle which juts into the water at Sutton pool." The place is now converted into a shipwright's yard, but some of the old buildings are said to be still in existence. In 1768 a patent was applied for and obtained by Cookworthy * " for a kind of porcelain newly invented, composed of moorstone or growan, and growan clay, the stone giving the ware transparence and mellowness, and the clay imparting whiteness and infusibility." It is evident from the wording of this document that Cookworthy clearly realised the mineralogical relation between china stone and china clay, and that these two materials were the essential ones required in a manufacture of porcelain like the Chinese. In a memorandum of his processes, which he appears to have completed at a later period, he gives most interesting details of his observations and experiments on the qualities of the materials procured from different districts, and of his difficulties in producing porcelain even after he had obtained considerable knowledge of the materials and their behaviour. He found that a mixture of equal parts of moor stone (china stone we now call it) and china clay gave very good results, for the paste or body of the porcelain, and that certain kinds of china stone made a sufficiently vitrifiable glaze without any admixture. In general use he adopted the method of glaze-making used by the Chinese, and fritted together a mixture of one part quicklime and two parts

* Patents Specifications, No. 898, March 17th, 1768.

Fig. 51.—SHELL-SHAPED SALT-CELLAR.
BRISTOL.

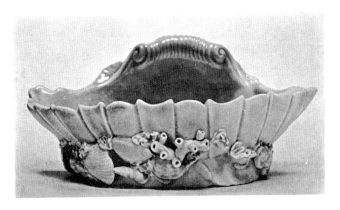

Fig. 52.— SHELL-SHAPED DESSERT-TRAY.
PLYMOUTH.

fern ashes, which was added to the china stone in proportions varying from one part of this frit with from ten to twenty parts of china stone. He adds that the proportion of one of frit to fifteen of stone was found most suitable. He was well aware that the Chinese dipped their vessels in the clay state and fired the glaze and body at one operation, but he remarks that it is very difficult to distinguish the proper thickness of the glaze in this way,* and his general method was to bake the shaped vessels to a soft biscuit, " so that they would suck," then paint them with blue if required, dip them in the glazing mixture, which readily dried on the biscuit ware, and fire the whole to the intense heat required to vitrify the glaze. This slight variation from the Chinese procedure does not in the least invalidate the claim of Plymouth porcelain to be considered as a " true " porcelain, for the final firing to melt the glaze must have been much more intense than that given to the body in the first case.

From his memoranda it is evident that various types of kiln and different fuels were tried for firing the ware, as he remarks that—

"The North of England† kilns, where the fire is applied on the outside of the kiln, the fuel is coal, will not do for our body. . . The only furnace or kiln, which we have tried with any degree of success, is the kiln used by the potters who make brown stone. It is called the 36-hole kiln. Wood is the fuel used in it. They burn billets before and under it, where there is an oven or arch pierced by 36 holes, through which the flame ascends into the chamber which contains the ware, and goes out at as many holes of the same dimensions in the crown of the furnace."‡

In the year 1768, when Cookworthy obtained his patent, he was 63 years of age, and however great his energy may have been, the multitude of little problems that had to be solved before

---

* Cookworthy's remarks on this point have been generally misunderstood by the writers of previous books on English porcelain.

† Probably Staffordshire.

‡ The oven here described by Cookworthy is precisely the same as that used at the Continental porcelain works, though Cookworthy does not seem to have been aware of that fact. It is figured on page 19 of Owen's " Two Centuries of Ceramic Art in Bristol," under the misleading designation of an " enamel kiln."

the manufacture could be perfected, were clearly beyond his strength. The difficulty of exactly proportioning the ingredients of body and glaze, of mastering the various processes of fabrication in a district remote from any established pottery works, and firing the ware so that it should be brought out of the oven bright and clear, and unstained by the smoke—everything, in fact, that distinguishes an established manufacture from an experimental one, must have told very heavily against the success of the Plymouth works, so that after a very short life they were abandoned and the business was removed to Bristol in 1770, where, under the care of a young and energetic man—Richard Champion —it developed into the famous Bristol porcelain works. Cookworthy and Lord Camelford are said to have lost some £3,000 in their venture at Plymouth, and how much of this sum they recovered by the transfer of the business and the patent rights to Champion is uncertain.

The existing pieces that can with certainty be attributed to the Plymouth factory are by no means numerous. They may be readily grouped into three classes, which may fairly be assumed to represent distinct stages in the development of the manufacture.

White pieces.—These comprise a few cups, generally of oval shape with leaf ornaments modelled in low relief, but the commonest pieces are salt-cellars in the shape of a shell, mounted on stands composed of smaller shells and corals. (*See* Fig. 52.) They are not very skilfully made or modelled, and are often stained with smoke. In the Schreiber collection there are several statuettes in the white state. A small one, described as "Frederick the Great," is indifferently modelled, and is deeply smoke-stained. Two larger figures of a gardener and his wife under *bocages* have all the quality of Plymouth porcelain, but the modelling and execution of the figures is very different to that of the early Plymouth pieces. In this case the smoke

PLATE XVIII.

Plymouth Vase,

WITH PAINTING IN ENAMEL COLOURS AND SLIGHT GILDING.

Prideaux Collection: Victoria and Albert Museum.

(*See pp.* 127-128.)

stain has communicated a warm grey tone to the glaze, which is artistically superior to what it would have been had it been properly fired.

Pieces decorated with painting in underglaze blue.—These pieces are often of the same form as the white pieces. Mugs, cups, saucers, sauce-boats, and shells are most commonly met with. The blue colour is generally very dark, quite blackish where thickly applied, and it is often " run " and streaky. Though Cookworthy is said to have invented a method of producing cobalt oxide from the ore, it cannot be said that his porcelain blue was remarkably good.

Enamelled pieces.—The same forms already mentioned, together with plates, teapots, vases, and a few figures, occur with enamel decorations of the style used in the early days of the other factories. The vase reproduced in Plate XVIII. is from the Prideaux collection in the Victoria and Albert Museum, and is a good example of the highest perfection ever reached at Plymouth. The shape is obviously imitated from the Chinese, and the little group of flowers, with butterflies and detached birds enamelled in brilliant colours, recalls the enamelling of early Chelsea pieces. It has been stated that a Frenchman from Sèvres, whose name is variously given as Sequoi, Soqui, or Le Quoi, was employed to design and direct the enamelling, but the work on the best pieces of enamelled Plymouth ware resembles that of Chelsea much more than that of Sèvres. A remarkable set of figures, emblematical of the four continents, was produced at Plymouth. One of these, the figure of Asia, is reproduced in Fig. 53. The modelling is extremely good, though the spotty enamelling on the robe detracts somewhat from the dignity of the figure. It is often difficult to decide whether any particular piece of this kind was made at Plymouth or at Bristol, as, no doubt, all the moulds were transferred to the latter place on the removal of the works.

The quality of the glaze at Plymouth, especially on the simple white, and blue and white pieces, is very characteristic. It is often greyish and full of bubbles, as well as being thick and uneven in patches owing to the fact that it had not been sufficiently fused to run level. The warm grey smoke stain has already been referred to, and, indeed, the glaze on the early pieces exhibits all the faults one would expect to find, considering the circumstances of its production. The superior quality of the glaze on the fine enamelled vases and other pieces has led to the suggestion that such pieces were not produced at the Plymouth factory, but at Bristol. Apart from the fact that many enamelled pieces are known in which the glaze is not of superlative excellence, it is only to be expected that the most perfect examples of glazing would be selected to receive the best enamel painting. The enamel painting is always in the form of floral sprays, and there are no instances known of the use of rich ground colours, though something of the kind was attempted, probably after the works were removed to Bristol. On the hard, infusible glaze the enamel colours stand up sharply, and are sometimes quite dry, having lost a portion of their flux to the glaze without appreciably softening into it.

Several instances of written inscriptions, such as " W. Cookworthy's factory, Plymouth," are recorded by Chaffers, but they are very exceptional. Only one mark is generally found on the pieces when a mark occurs at all, and this is the alchemical symbol for tin, which resembles the Arabic numerals 2 and 4 conjoined. It occurs painted in underglaze blue on the blue and white pieces, and in red or reddish brown enamel on the enamelled pieces. A few of the best pieces on which gold has been used in the decoration have the mark in gold, but it appears probable that the more elaborate pieces bearing the mark in gold were made at the Bristol factory of Cookworthy and Co.

FIG. 53. – FIGURE OF "ASIA."
PLYMOUTH.

CHAPTER XII.

THE term "Bristol porcelain " is generally understood to mean the productions of the factory which was established by William Cookworthy and Co. at 15, Castle Green, when the Plymouth business was removed to this city in 1770, and which was afterwards transferred to Richard Champion, who carried it on until 1781. It has long been suspected from the existence of a few pieces differing from the ordinary wares of this factory that there must have been some earlier attempts at porcelain making in Bristol. There are, for instance, a few sauce-boats known which have the word " Bristoll " in raised letters under the foot ; there are also a few pieces believed, on very good authority, to have been made by John Britain or Brittan, who was Champion's foreman. Of these a plate had the inscription " J. B. 1753," a bowl was dated 1762 (both these specimens were roughly painted in blue), and a cup is also in existence with the Britain arms painted in colours. Nothing has hitherto been known of the site of the works where these pieces were made, or of any person concerned in the manufacture, apart from Britain himself. Mr. R. L. Hobson, of the British Museum, has drawn our attention to some statements made by Dr. Richard Pococke, Bishop of Meath and Ossory, whose letters, descriptive of his tours through England in 1750–1751, have been issued by the Camden Society. Writing from Bristol on November 2nd, 1750, he says : *

* " Dr. Pococke's Travels Through England During the Years 1750–1751." Two volumes. Camden Society, 1888. Vol. I., p. 159.

J

I went to see a manufacture lately established here by one of the principal of the manufacture at Lime House which failed. It is at a glass house and is called Lowris (?) China House. They have two sorts of ware, one called Stone China, which has a yellow cast, both in the ware and the glazing, that I suppose is made of pipeclay and calcined flint. The other they call old China ; this is whiter, and I suppose this is made of calcined flint and the *soapy rock* at Lizard Point, which 'tis known they use. . . *They make very beautiful white sauce-boats, adorned with reliefs of festoons, which sell for sixteen shillings a pair.*

This remark about the soapy rock at Lizard Point is explained by reference to an earlier letter in the same volume dated October 13th, 1750,* where he says :

We went nine miles to the south (from Helston) near as far as Lizard Point, to see the Soapy rock, which is a little opening in the cliff, where a rivulet runs over a vein of soapy rock into the sea . . . there are white patches in it, which is mostly valued for making porcelain, and they get five pounds a ton for it, for the manufacture of porcelain now carrying on at Bristol . . . it feels like soap, and being so dear it must be much better than pipeclay ; there is a vein of something of the like nature at the Lizard Point.

This information is of the utmost importance, for it proves that soapy rock or soap-stone was used for porcelain-making at a much earlier date than has hitherto been suspected, and, further, that sauce-boats were being made at Bristol in 1750 by a man from the works at Limehouse, London, of which we have no other information than is furnished by similar incidental references. In Fig. 54 will be found an illustration of a sauce-boat in the British Museum, which has the word " Bristoll " in raised letters under the foot. This specimen is of a white opaque body, exactly such as could be obtained from a mixture of flint and soapy rock, and after reading the Bishop's account of the " very beautiful white sauce-boats adorned with reliefs of festoons," there can be no doubt that here is one of the pieces made at this early factory. We have no further information of the venture or of how it progressed, but the companion sauce-boat (Fig. 55) shows us, at all events, that something from this factory went to the building up of Champion's business more than

* *Opus cit.*, Vol. I., p. 120.

Fig. 54.—White sauce-boat
(marked "Bristoll").
BRISTOL.

Fig. 55.—Sauce-boat with festoons in green
("Bristoll" mark disguised).
BRISTOL.

twenty years afterwards. The second sauce-boat, which is also in the British Museum, is a true porcelain, having all the qualities generally associated with the ordinary productions of Champion's factory. It is obviously made from an identical mould, and the word " Bristoll " also occurs in raised letters under the foot. The " reliefs of festoons " have, however, been covered with the characteristic enamel green of Champion's ware, and a green leaf has been painted over the raised " Bristoll " in order to disguise it. It seems obvious that Champion bought the moulds of this first little works, and made pieces from them, but, in order to give his pieces a somewhat different character, painted the modelled ornament and disguised the impressed mark. It is extremely unlikely that this first manufacture ever attained any position of importance, but established, as it apparently was, in connection with a glass house, it may have been carried on in a small way for years by a few workmen and without the intervention of a capitalist. The potter's art owes much to little ventures such as this, where two or three men working on their own account have carried on a business for years, making little progress financially, but gaining knowledge by experiment, and laying the foundations of practical experience on which the larger factories were successfully built by men of better commercial instincts.

John Britain was in all probability one of the workmen at this factory, and here he obtained the practical acquaintance with china-making that qualified him for the position of foreman in Champion's later works.

The next fragment of information we possess that throws any light on the history of Bristol porcelain is connected with a box of the Cherokee clay (a china clay from Carolina) that Champion received from his American correspondent, Caleb Lloyd, in 1765, with a request that he would have it tried for porcelain-making. Replying in 1766, Champion says that he had obtained a trial of this clay " at a manufactory set up here some time ago, on the principle of the Chinese porcelain, but not being successful, is now given up." In a previous letter written in 1765 he speaks of this works as "newly established," and in February, 1766, as being "now given up," so that it is possible this was not the works which had been in operation in 1750, 1753, and 1762; or, if it was, then it could only have been "newly established" to Champion. It is perfectly clear from this correspondence that Champion had no connection with the manufacture of porcelain in 1766, and though it has been suggested that he commenced operations in 1768, there is no evidence for such a theory, neither is there any trace of a porcelain factory, of any size or importance, in Bristol until the end of 1770, when, as has been already stated, the Plymouth business was removed to Bristol and established at what is now 15, Castle Green. An examination of the Bristol rate books* has shown that from September, 1771, to September, 1773, these premises were rated as a " china manufactory carried on by Wm. Cookworthy and Co." Cookworthy was at this time (1770) sixty-five years of age, and though he was a man of great activity, and was in Bristol in June, and again at Christmas in that year, it was not to be expected that he could exercise an active supervision of the works. We have no direct information as to what persons were associated with him in the undertaking, but it is conceivable that a young, active, ambitious man like Champion, who was a merchant in the American trade, and had received a commercial training, would be a very likely man for Cookworthy to turn to, especially if Champion, as is stated, had retained some interest in the question of porcelain making after receiving the sample of Cherokee clay. At all events, we know that the Plymouth business was continued at Castle Green, and it appears that, after the removal to Bristol, pieces of more elaborate and more perfect technique were produced. Speaking broadly, the wares of the Plymouth factory were strongly tinged with the Oriental influence, but the pieces which are attributed to the Bristol factory of W. Cookworthy and Co. show just as strongly the influence of the Dresden style, which, as we shall see, was the ideal at which Champion aimed. A few advertisements of the productions of the factory during the

---

* Owen's " Two Centuries of Ceramic Art in Bristol," p. 20.

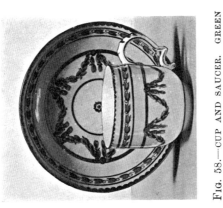

FIG. 58.—CUP AND SAUCER. GREEN AND GOLD ENAMELLING. **BRISTOL.**

FIG. 57.—TWO-HANDLED COVERED CUP AND SAUCER. **BRISTOL.**

FIG. 56.—CUP AND SAUCER. IMPRESSED SCALE PATTERN, AND PAINTED BORDER. **BRISTOL.**

years 1771–1773 have been found in Felix Farley's *Bristol Journal*, and Sarah Farley's *Bristol Journal*. The advertisements speak of "Figures, vases, jars, and beakers, which are very elegant, and the useful ware exceedingly good." We are also told that the body equals the "East Indian," and the decorations the "Dresden," "which this work more particularly imitates"—a further proof, if proof be needed, that Champion was interested, probably as managing partner, in the firm of Wm. Cookworthy and Co., from its first settlement in Bristol. It is difficult to speak with absolute certainty of the productions of the factory during this period, but it is generally agreed that the richly decorated vases and tea and coffee pots, which bear the usual Plymouth mark, but in gold, were made at this time.

The most readily accessible of these, to the ordinary student, are the three fine pieces in the Schreiber collection, consisting of a very elaborately decorated teapot and coffee pot of large size, and a more simply decorated and somewhat smaller teapot. These pieces remained for a long time in the Cookworthy family, and they were traditionally believed to have been made at Plymouth ; it is, however, now held that they were made at Bristol, but while Cookworthy still retained an interest in the factory there. In the two larger pieces the ground is of blue, veined with darker lines and patches of the same colour, very much as a house-painter would do imitation marbling.* Evidently the idea was to produce richly broken blue colour like that found on old Chelsea and Worcester pieces, but as the colour of these Bristol pieces is painted over the glaze and not under it, the effect is poor and thin. White panels are reserved on the body of the pieces to receive paintings of floral sprays in enamel colours, and these panels are bordered by gilt scrolls. The result, however, is one of elaboration rather than of richness, and the overglaze colours stand up on the glaze, producing a hard, dry effect, which shows how ill adapted the

---

* It is interesting to notice that the same device was being used on Derby-Chelsea vases at the same period, though the veining was sometimes done with gold. The stand of the Derby-Chelsea vase (Fig. 16) is decorated in this way.

colours and methods of painting of the glassy porcelain factories were when applied to the refractory glaze of a true porcelain. Other pieces decorated in an equally elaborate manner are known, but as to the ordinary productions of the factory during this period, such as the " useful " ware mentioned in the advertisements, we have very little information. The common ware would certainly not be marked in gold, and so few pieces are known bearing the Plymouth mark in addition to that of Bristol, that we are unable to form any definite conclusions from them.

It seems possible that Champion may have contemplated the purchase of Cookworthy's patent, or of an interest in it, as early as 1768, and in 1772 he must have been in treaty for the business, as he began to take apprentices, of whom the first was Henry Bone, afterwards famous as a miniature painter and enameller on metal.* In the indentures of the apprentices during the years 1772–1773 Champion is described as a china manufacturer, and there is no doubt that with the pecuniary support of certain wealthy friends, he obtained a preponderating influence in the business, and ultimately was able to secure the entire patent rights of Cookworthy. The title of the firm was changed from Wm. Cookworthy and Co. to Richard Champion and Co. in 1773, and though all the legal formalities attending the transfer do not appear to have been completed till May, 1774, the entire business was in Champion's hands from September, 1773, at least. Had Champion devoted the whole of his time and strength to the manufacture of porcelain, there can be no doubt that he would have made it a commercial success, for he was a man of ability ; but he seems to have spread his energies over too wide a field, with the result that none of his affairs really prospered. He was primarily an American merchant, and not a potter, and the unsettled state of affairs in the years

* Henry Bone, R.A., was born at Truro in 1755. His parents removed to Plymouth, and he is said to have been employed by Cookworthy, but in what capacity is unknown. He can hardly have been employed as a painter at Plymouth, for he was only fifteen when the business was removed to Bristol. He was apprenticed to Champion on January 20th, 1772, for seven years, and left at the end of his apprenticeship. He was elected an A.R.A. in 1802 and R.A. in 1811

PLATE XIX.

BRISTOL PORCELAIN.

Cup and Saucer of typical Bristol Pattern.

SAID TO HAVE BEEN DECORATED BY HENRY BONE.

Two-handled Covered Cup and Saucer.

PAINTED WITH VIEW OF PLAS NEWYDD, THE COTTAGE OF THE
LADIES OF LLANGOLLEN.

British Museum.

(*See p.* 140.)

immediately preceding the American War of Independence involved him in serious business troubles and losses. At the same time he was an ardent politician, and was largely responsible for inducing Edmund Burke to come forward as a candidate for the representation of Bristol at the general election of 1774. As he also busied himself greatly in local affairs, it will be realised that he had hardly the time or energy left to perfect a new and difficult industry. It is very probable that these difficulties had involved him in heavy expenditure, and, relying on the support of Edmund Burke, he endeavoured, in 1775, to obtain an extension of the original Cookworthy patent, doubtless in the hope that he might thus recoup the losses sustained in the early years of the undertaking. Burke did everything for Champion's success that interest or friendship could have dictated, and there is little doubt that Champion would have obtained the sole right to the use of china stone and china clay for fourteen years beyond the period of Cookworthy's original patent, but for the opposition of Josiah Wedgwood. Many writers on the history of Bristol porcelain have stated that Wedgwood's opposition was marked by bitterness and unfairness, but it is difficult to see how such charges can be sustained. When Champion purchased the patent rights from Cookworthy, he did so with the knowledge that the patent would expire in a given number of years, and Wedgwood naturally objected to the proposal that he and his fellow earthenware manufacturers in Staffordshire should be debarred from using china stone and china clay in their productions, except on payment of excessive royalties to a man who was not developing a process that he had invented or discovered, but who was speculating in the fruits of other people's experiments. It certainly seems that the fullest justice was done when Champion was allowed an extension of the patent for the use of china stone and china clay in porcelain, the only substance ever produced by Cookworthy or Champion, and the other potters of the country were allowed to use the same materials in earthenware bodies. However much Champion may have owed to the friendly support of such prominent

members of the Whig party as Edmund Burke, the Duke of Portland, the Marquis of Rockingham, Earl Fitzwilliam and others,
the cost of obtaining the Act of Parliament extending his patent
undoubtedly proved a heavy drain on his resources. To add to
his difficulties, the storm that had been so long brewing in the
Colonies burst, and with the outbreak of the war Champion's
business as an American merchant must have been practically
extinguished. The state of trade throughout the country was
deplorable, and Bristol, which had such intimate connections with
the Colonies, must have suffered more than other towns. But for
the assistance of friends who knew his worth, Champion might
have been entirely ruined, yet, though his business as a merchant
was at an end, he carried on the china works for a few years longer.
In 1776 a London warehouse was opened at 17, Salisbury Court,
Fleet Street ; and it seems possible that Edmund Burke was concerned in this branch of the business.* In the same year Champion
was desirous of obtaining a partner who could bring in capital to
extend the business, but the times were unfavourable, and no
such enterprising person was found. It seems probable that the
best period of the works lasted from 1776 to 1778, and that by
the end of the latter year Champion began to think of disposing of
his factory and his patent rights. It was not, however, until
1781 that he succeeded in selling his patent rights to a company
of seven Staffordshire potters, who commenced the manufacture
of true porcelain at Tunstall. Champion removed to Staffordshire
in November, 1781, but in April, 1782, he seems to have left Staffordshire for London. Burke appointed him Deputy Paymaster
of the Forces, but he only held this appointment for a few months
—April to July, 1782—and again under the Coalition Ministry of
1783. He emigrated to America in October 1784, and died at
Rocky Branch, near Camden, South Carolina, in October, 1791, at
the comparatively early age of forty-eight. It is impossible to close
this brief account of his career without expressing regret that a
man of such ability as Champion undoubtedly possessed, should

* *See* Owen, *opus cit.*, p. 189.

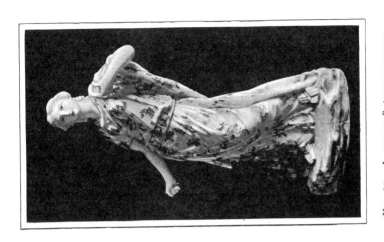

FIG. 60.—"AUTUMN"; (ONE OF GROUP OF CLASSIC SEASONS).

BRISTOL.

FIG. 59.—"WATER"; (ONE OF GROUP OF CLASSIC ELEMENTS).

BRISTOL.

have been overwhelmed by misfortune. It is, however, perfectly clear that his own sanguine and eager temperament and his love of politics largely contributed to his downfall. He was not a potter, and can have had little acquaintance with the technical details of the manufacture. Apparently he was more anxious to produce expensive pieces decorated in the Dresden manner than to adopt the humbler but safer course of making simple articles like the early wares of Worcester, and he paid the penalty of his inexperience or his ambition.

The articles produced by the factory during the seven or eight years—1773–1781—when it was under the control of Champion can be arranged, for purposes of study, into well-marked groups. The simplest comprise what is known as "Champion's Cottage China," the ordinary useful china made in the true Chinese fashion by firing body and glaze at one operation. The shapes and the decorations of these pieces are always simple, but it is curious that so few of them should have been painted with underglaze blue. When they are decorated, the ornament generally takes the form of roughly painted sprays of flowers, occasionally with festooned riband borders. The enamel colours themselves are very poor indeed, being thin in quality and hard and dry in texture, from the nature of the glaze on which they were applied. Gilding seems not to have been used on this variety of Champion's porcelain. In addition to useful ware, a few small statuettes of children were produced in the cottage china, but they are poorly modelled, as a rule, and almost rudely daubed with colour. It cannot be said that this cottage china adds much to the reputation of the factory, though it seems to have been produced in its later days, and not, as one might have expected, at the beginning of its history. Had Champion contented himself at first with making this commoner ware, and then gradually built up a business for better finished and more highly decorated goods, his works might have been more successful; but he seems to have only tried to develop this simple ware when it was already too late, and his pecuniary losses had exhausted his capital.

The more elaborate and highly finished productions of Champion's factory seem to have been made after the plan adopted by Cookworthy at Plymouth.* The body was first fired to an easy " biscuit " state, so that it would be almost as absorbent and as fragile as a clay tobacco pipe ; it was then dipped in the glaze and refired at a much higher temperature. Various mixtures were used at different times for the body and the glaze, and Champion, in filing his specification as required by the Act of Parliament granting an extension of Cookworthy's patent, mentions many proportions in which the materials might be used for his purposes. Professor Church has given a most careful and accurate account of the composition and physical properties of the Bristol porcelain, which shows that in hardness and infusibility the ware ranks higher than either Dresden or Chinese. The amount of alkalies in the paste is exceptionally low, and consequently a very fierce heat must have been required to bring the ware to perfection. It has been rather hastily assumed by many writers, because the wares of Plymouth and Bristol needed such a high temperature in their baking, that the manufacture must have been more difficult and costly than that of the glassy porcelains of Chelsea, Bow, and Worcester. Such an idea is quite destitute of foundation, and there can be no doubt that the glassy porcelains were much more difficult of production, owing to the narrow limits of temperature within which they could be safely fired, and to the great change in the fusibility of the mass caused by relatively trifling variations in the mixtures used. The thrown ware produced at Plymouth and Bristol often exhibits the well-known defect called by pottery workmen " wreathing," that is, the appearance of spiral ridges running round the pieces from bottom to top. It has been assumed by Owen, in his account of the Bristol factory, that true porcelain is specially liable to this defect, but this is erroneous, as is also the description given by the same writer of the cause of the defect. It is really due to bad " throwing," and its frequent occurrence proves that the throwers employed at these factories were not always

* *See* pp. 124-125.

FIG. 63.—"SUMMER"—RUSTIC FIGURE.
BRISTOL.

FIG. 62.—GIRL WITH TRIANGLE.
BRISTOL.

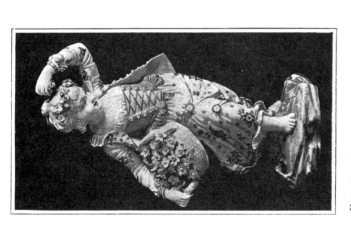

FIG. 61.—"SPRING." RUSTIC FIGURE.
BRISTOL.

first-rate workmen—a very natural state of affairs when we consider the situation of the factories, and the fact that the materials used differed from those of the other factories, and required somewhat different manipulation.

The known examples of Champion's manufacture reveal the influence of a variety of decorative styles. We have already referred to the sauce-boats (Fig. 55) made from the moulds of the first Bristol factory, and it is not uncommon to find pieces that were probably made from Plymouth moulds, or in continuation of Plymouth traditions. The statuettes representing the "four continents," which were produced at Plymouth (*see* Fig. 53) were also made at Bristol; and in Fig. 51 a Bristol shell-shaped salt-cellar is shown on the same page as an earlier and ruder Plymouth specimen. The paramount influence at Bristol was, however, that of Dresden, and not only were the shapes and ornamental devices of that factory copied, but the mark of the crossed swords seems to have been extensively used—a piece of forgery for which there can be no defence.

The catalogue of the 1780 sale of the output of the Bristol factory, specifically mentions " Elegant patterns in Desert Services, Tea and Coffee Equipages, Cabinet and Caudle cups," and it seems probable that the commercial productions of the factory largely consisted of articles of this description. Three excellent examples of such ware are reproduced in Figs. 56–58. The two-handled cup with slight festoons of flowers is lighter and more elegant in style than the majority of Bristol pieces. The cup and saucer decorated with rather heavy festoons of green laurel and with simple gilding represents a style of decoration that seems to have been very much used. The green enamel employed in the painting of these festoons is the only enamel colour that fires to a glossy surface on the hard Bristol glaze. It is so brilliant and transparent and was such a favourite colour, that it is almost distinctive of the productions of the factory. The cup and saucer, with an embossed " pine-cone " or " scale " pattern, may be compared with similar pieces made at Bow, Worcester, Chelsea, and Derby (*see* Figs. 18 and

21), but the painted border, which recalls the treatment of Oriental borders found on Rouen faience, is more characteristic of Bristol. Without the trivial little spray of flowers in the well of the saucer, this cup and saucer would have been perfectly decorated. On Plate XIX. will be found illustrations in colour of more elaborate cups and saucers. The cylindrical cup with its saucer decorated with green laurel festoons, enclosing medallions, with paintings of antique subjects in *grisaille* on a chocolate ground, is typical of another style of decoration which was evidently popular, as a number of such pieces are mentioned in the sale catalogue already referred to. The specimens here shown are from the British Museum, and are said to have been painted by Henry Bone during his connection with the factory. The covered cup and saucer (also from the British Museum) has an unusually well-designed pattern upon it. It is further interesting from the fact that it was made for " The Ladies of Llangollen," and bears a painting of their cottage in the reserved medallion. It would be very interesting to know if the ladies were responsible for the design on the piece, as it is quite unlike the general style in vogue at Bristol.

The most elaborate Bristol tea services are those connected with Edmund Burke. The first of these was made in 1774 for Burke to present to the wife of Mr. Joseph Smith, at whose house in Bristol he had resided during the election contest of that year. The pieces are in the Dresden style, decorated with the usual festoons in green laurel, and with slighter ornament in gold. The medallions bear the arms of the family and the initials of Mrs. Smith (" S. S."), painted in tiny flowers. The second service was made during the same year, and was a present from Champion and his wife to Mrs. Burke. From an artistic point of view the pieces of this service are most unsatisfactory. The central feature of the design is a pedestal bearing a shield emblazoned with the arms of Burke impaling Nugent ; above this pedestal is a little figure of Hymen with a torch, and for supporters two figures representing respectively " Liberty " holding a Phrygian cap on a spear, and a shield with the gorgon's head, and " Plenty," with a cornucopia. In

PLATE XX.

BRISTOL PORCELAIN.

Hexagonal Vase.

WITH YELLOW GROUND OF EXCEPTIONAL QUALITY.

British Museum.

(See pp. 141-142.*)*

addition to this, there are wreaths of roses, scales of justice, and hands of friendship clasping a caduceus, so that one wonders what the author of the essay on "The Origin of our Ideas on the Sublime and Beautiful" thought of it all.

Several sets of figures were produced at Bristol, and some of them were exceedingly well modelled and very prettily decorated. Groups representing "The Four Seasons" and "The Elements," in the shape of classic figures each about 10 inches high, are well known. Fig. 59 is the figure of "Water" from the elements series, and Fig. 60 is the "Autumn" from the set of the seasons. Although these figures are somewhat distorted from inefficient "propping" during the firing, they are finely conceived and very well made. The prettiest, however, are found among the sets known as the "Rustic Seasons," and the rarer "Music Figures." We illustrate the "Spring" and "Summer" of the former series, and the "Girl with Triangle" of the latter, from examples in the Schreiber collection. The best Bristol figures often bear the mark "T°" impressed in the paste, and this is supposed to be the mark of the modeller Tebo. It must be said, however, that many of them are imitated from well-known Dresden figures; and a glance at the figures of the "Rustic Seasons" reveals the Dresden style of the enamelling. With the characteristic cold glitter of the Bristol glaze, and the dry enamel colours, there is no difficulty in separating the figures of this factory from those of Chelsea, Bow, or Derby.

A few large and important vases are known which were undoubtedly produced at Bristol, as many of them remained in the possession of the Fry family from the time they left the works. They are hexagonal in shape, standing about a foot high, or such of them as have covers, about sixteen inches to the top of the cover. The shape is obviously Oriental, but the decoration is generally drawn from a mixture of Oriental and Dresden motives. Some of them, for instance, are painted with exotic birds, but in others the ornament consists of modelled masks, festoons of flowers, bows of ribbon, or large leaves springing from the base, or hanging down the angles and across the panels. An unusual and very fine example is in the British Museum (*see* Plate XX.), and in the Schreiber collection is one painted with birds. The British Museum specimen is remarkable for its splendid yellow enamel ground, which is of finer and richer quality than the yellow grounds of Worcester and Derby, and also for its skilfully drawn sprays of conventional foliage in a warm purple brown. The use of the applied masks and modelled flower festoons is also shown on this same piece, which is possibly the finest in existence.

A more refined and distinctive form of modelled flower work in porcelain is confined to the Bristol factory. This is found in the delicately modelled flower pieces in biscuit porcelain, where the artificial petals are almost as delicate as the real ones they imitate. The sprays of flowers were applied to oval or circular medallions which seem to have been made in two sizes, about three inches and about six inches in diameter. There are a few medallions known, generally of the larger size, in which the flowers and leaves form a wreath round an embossed coat of arms, or a portrait in relief. Although they are mostly in pure white biscuit porcelain, one or two have been found which have the arms picked out in rich, dead gold. Mr. Owen has recorded a number of these medallions with coats of arms, notably pieces bearing respectively the arms of France, of Elton impaling Tierney, of Harford impaling Lloyd, and of Burke impaling Nugent. Fig. 64 is a reproduction of the last-mentioned, which was probably presented to Mrs. Burke along with the tea service already described ; it is now preserved in the British Museum. The largest known piece of this kind is a plaque, also in the British Museum, bearing in the centre a medallion portrait of Benjamin Franklin. It has been suggested that pieces of this class were only made as presents to personal friends of Champion's, and never for sale like the plaques decorated with flowers only.

The best known mark on Champion's productions is a cross. It occurs incised in the paste, painted in blue generally under the glaze, and also in gold over the glaze. Another mark is the letter " B." These marks are often accompanied by a numeral, in gold

FIG. 64.—BISCUIT PORCELAIN, PLAQUE.
THE ARMS OF BURKE IMPALING
NUGENT ; WITH A WREATH OF
FLOWERS.
BRISTOL.

or colour, which is supposed to be the distinguishing mark of the painter. The use of the Dresden mark has already been referred to ; it is generally in underglaze blue, and is sometimes partly disguised by other marks painted over the glaze subsequently. The alchemical symbol for tin when it occurs in gold on richly decorated pieces is supposed to mark the productions of the Bristol factory while it belonged to W. Cookworthy and Co.

CHAPTER XIII.

CAUGHLEY AND COALPORT.

A POTTERY works is said to have been established at Caughley a few miles above Bridgenorth, on the right bank of the Severn and some distance up from the river, as early as 1751 ; but no porcelain was produced there until Thomas Turner came from Worcester in or about 1772, and took an interest in the works of which he afterwards became sole proprietor. Turner had apparently been an engraver at Worcester, and one of the things for which Caughley was noted was the excellence of its blue printed ware. In speaking of the use of printing at Worcester, we have said that the early patterns were printed on the fired glaze. Printing in underglaze colours must have presented many difficulties, and even when it was perfected, blue was the only colour used for a long time. We cannot say that blue-printed porcelain originated at Caughley, but many of the best early examples undoubtedly came from this works. It was here that two patterns were devised, about 1780, that have been more largely used in the decoration of the cheaper kinds of English porcelain than any other half-dozen patterns combined. These were the " willow pattern " and the " Broseley dragon," both owing their inception to Chinese designs, but produced in a manner that no Chinaman ever dreamt of. In Fig. 65 will be found an illustration of a small tray of Caughley porcelain with an early form of the " willow pattern," and above it a mustard-pot (Fig. 66) with another printed pattern which is equally imitative of Oriental design. There is no doubt that during the first ten years or so of the factory the ware produced was mainly of this kind, and it is interesting to compare the pieces of

FIG. 65.—MUSTARD POT, PRINTED IN
UNDER-GLAZE BLUE.
CAUGHLEY.

FIG. 66.—TRAY, PRINTED IN UNDER-GLAZE
BLUE.
CAUGHLEY.

this period with the blue and white pieces of Worcester. The Oriental influence was strongly marked at both factories, but the Worcester pieces are much nearer in quality to the original. The Caughley body is whiter and more translucent than that of Worcester, and the blue is also brighter, so that there is really less of that harmony between the colour and the ground which gives such subtle charm to the best Chinese blue and white porcelain. It is certain that the brightness of the colour and the sharpness of the engraving of this porcelain soon gave Turner a considerable trade in articles for domestic use, and a London warehouse, known as the " Salopian China Warehouse," was opened at 5, Portugal Street, Lincoln's Inn Fields, about 1780.

In detailing the history of the Worcester factories it has been stated that when the Chamberlains left the old works in 1783 or 1784 and founded a rival business, they obtained their porcelain from the Caughley works, and continued to do so down to 1789 at least. Naturally they required shapes as much like those of the parent Worcester factory as possible, and this, coupled with the fact that Turner came from Worcester, will account for the close resemblance in form between many of the Caughley shapes and those of Worcester.

Certain distinctive shapes must have been made at Caughley before 1780, however, as in the sale of Champion's Bristol china which took place in that year one of the lots is described as " One complete Salopian table set, 126 pieces, the new Salopian sprigs," and another as "A Salopian table service with Chantille sprigs, containing 115 pieces." It is unlikely that these were of actual Caughley manufacture, but the works here must have come rapidly into prominence if their productions were so soon imitated at Bristol. Turner is said to have paid a visit to France in 1780, and to have brought back with him several artists and workmen from some of the French factories. Whatever truth there may be in this legend, it is known that some time after 1780 rich gilding was produced at Caughley, and pieces are often met with having portions of the design in the bright underglaze blue, and the finer details worked

K

out in gold. Generally, in these pieces, the blue takes the form of flowers or bands, and the gilding that of delicate sprays of foliage springing from or enclosing the blue. Some pieces bore painted landscapes, floral designs, and sprays with birds, generally executed in on-glaze colours. It has frequently been remarked that in these pieces the work often resembles that on contemporary Derby wares. Mr. Jewitt, indeed, states that the Derby flower painter, Withers (who painted the Rodney jug), was employed at Caughley in 1795, while it is also known that Thomas Martin Randall, who served his apprenticeship at Caughley and was a famous bird painter there, afterwards worked at Derby. If the productions of the Caughley works have little artistic importance, the works will always be of interest, as, apart from the great development of blue printing already mentioned, it played the part of foster-parent to Chamberlain's venture ; while John Rose, the founder of the Coalport Works, and Thomas Minton, the founder of the firm which was to develop into the world-famous house of " Mintons," were both trained there.

Turner retired from business in 1799, and the works was sold to John Rose, who carried it on mainly for the production of biscuit china, which was decorated at Coalport. The business seems to have been gradually transferred to the newer works, and in 1814 or 1815 the Caughley works was entirely dismantled and the materials removed to Coalport on the opposite side of the Severn, and there used for the erection of additional buildings. The site of the old works, which when visited this year was covered with waving crops, is still known as Factory Field.

The first mark used at Caughley was probably a " C," generally printed in blue. It often, however, closely resembles the crescent mark of Worcester, and it has been suggested that the " C " was used for that reason. Another early mark is a painted or printed " S," also in blue, which probably stood for the initial letter of the word " Salopian." Later, the word " SALOPIAN " was often impressed in the paste, and the painted " S " and " C " marks were occasionally used in conjunction with this mark. In addition to

FIG. 67.—VASE. PERFORATED WORK.
COALPORT.

these marks a series of Arabic numerals (from 1 to 8), with various flourishes to disguise them, are known. Of these the disguised "5," painted in underglaze blue, seems to be of most frequent occurrence.

COALPORT.

The .well-known Coalport China Factory situated on the left bank of the Severn, about two miles below Ironbridge, and almost opposite the Caughley works, owed its long-continued success to John Rose, its first manager, and ultimately its proprietor. This John Rose had been originally connected with the Caughley works, but he appears to have left there about 1780, and commenced a little business on his own account at Jackfield in the immediate neighbourhood.* About 1790 he removed his works to Coalport, a mile lower down the river, and on the opposite bank, where there was a newly opened canal, which brought coal down to the Severn. A small works had already been established here by Thomas Rose (John Rose's brother), and partners, under the title of " Anstice, Rose and Horton," and the two little works were carried on independently for some time, with the canal between them. John Rose seems to have been an enterprising business man, and he soon amalgamated the two firms, and then, in 1799, purchased the Caughley works, which he had left nearly twenty years before. The business seems to have prospered from the first, and large quantities of ware were turned out not only in continuation of the Caughley productions, but also in direct imitation of Sèvres and Dresden pieces, which still exercised a powerful influence on English porcelain.

Coalport, possibly from its situation in one of the most picturesque parts of the Severn valley, seems to have had great attractions for the painters of other factories, and men came from Worcester, Derby, and the Staffordshire potteries, bringing with them all the current styles of those places. Thus, the famous deep " ground-laid " Mazarine blue of Derby, which has already been

* It is believed that the site of this Jackfield works of John Rose's was a portion of that now occupied by the works of Craven, Dunnill and Company, Limited.

referred to,* was soon reproduced at Coalport, and it is difficult to say which of the two factories produced the deeper, richer, and more velvety colour. The use of elaborate decoration in raised flowers was also brought from Derby in the same way, and, indeed, there was hardly a process or a style of decoration used in England that did not make its appearance on Coalport porcelain. That the works was carried on with enterprise is shown by the fact that John Rose, finding his trade with one of the great London dealers diminished by the sale of the porcelain produced at Nantgarw by Billingsley and Walker,† went down into South Wales and brought these workmen over to Coalport to make their famous ware for him. They were no more successful in this enterprise at Coalport than they had been elsewhere, and their process was soon abandoned as being too uncertain, and consequently too costly. It is probable that such porcelain as was made at Coalport from this receipt had the word " Nantgarw " impressed in the paste.

Rose's efforts did not stop here, as in 1820 he was awarded the " Isis " Gold Medal of the Society of Arts for having produced the best china glaze for painting upon, free from lead or any other compound deleterious to the health of the workpeople. This glaze resembled the glaze of true porcelain in so far as it had a felspathic basis, but it was made to fuse at a lower temperature by the addition of a large proportion of borax and some silicate of soda and potash. The great practical advantage it possessed over the " true " porcelain glaze was that it required far less heat to melt it, and that, owing to its more ready fusibility, the enamel colours when painted on it and fired in the kiln, sank into the glaze and became incorporated with it, just as would have been the case with a soft lead glaze. About the same period he also commenced to use pure felspar in the body of his porcelain, following the example of Spode, and pieces are often met with bearing the inscription " Coalport Improved Feltspar Porcelain." This improvement of his body and glaze apparently encouraged him still further in the production of pieces in deliberate imitation of the old wares of

* *See* p. 98.　　　　　† *See* p. 164.

Fig. 68.— COVERED CUP AND SAUCER.
IMITATION SÈVRES STYLE.
COALPORT.

Fig. 69.— PLATE OF THE CZAR'S SERVICE (1851)
COALPORT.

Chelsea and Sèvres, and, not content with imitating their shapes and decorations, he even copied the mark of the gold anchor of the one and the crossed " L's " of the other.

From 1820 to 1860 the works prospered exceedingly, and was one of the largest and busiest china works in the country. John Rose died in 1841, and the business was continued under the old title of " John Rose and Co.," by his nephew, W. F. Rose, and Mr. William Pugh. In 1862 William Pugh became sole proprietor of the works, and continued so to his death in 1875. Shortly after this time the business was thrown into Chancery by Pugh's executors, and a receiver was appointed to manage the factory. This resulted in an enormous amount of old Coalport stock, that had accumulated on the premises, being decorated and sold off. The business had been reduced to a low ebb when it was acquired by the " Coalport China Company," who now carry on the works on the old site.

It is difficult to speak of any particular Coalport style in the period with which this history is concerned—*i.e.* down to 1850. When direct imitation of the styles of other factories is even partially attempted, the resultant influence is felt on all the output of a works. So it was at Coalport, and there is no pleasure in recounting how they succeeded in producing inferior copies of Chelsea, Sèvres, Dresden, Worcester, and Derby pieces. The production of the dark Mazarine blue has been already alluded to, and the imitation of Sèvres led to the search for the rich ground colours for which that factory had been so famous. Walker, of Nantgarw, is said to have introduced a deep maroon colour, and large sums of money were expended in attempts to rival the famous " Sèvres turquoise." For a long time nothing better than a pale and feeble imitation, known as " celeste," was obtained ; finally a much better colour was produced, but even this is never equal to that of the " Vieux Sèvres " itself. In 1850, it is said, at the instigation of Messrs. Daniell, the London dealers, the famous rose-du-Barri, or rose Pompadour, ground was obtained for the first time in England, though the well-known claret colour of

Chelsea and a pink ground produced at Derby are evidence of earlier efforts in the same direction.

The illustrations of Coalport pieces given are taken from specimens formerly in the Jermyn Street Museum, now temporarily housed at Bethnal Green. The open-work vase and cover (Fig. 67) is a good example of the lengths to which flower work was carried, the entire piece being made to represent flowers with their leaves and stalks. The piece is heavy in design, and is very crudely decorated with colours and gold. It compares unfavourably with the use of " flowering " at the earlier English factories. This piece is marked " Coalport " in underglaze blue. Of the direct copies of Sèvres pieces the cup and saucer in Fig. 68, with their turquoise ground, rich gilding, and painted birds, is a very good example. It is marked with the crossed " L's " of Sèvres, in blue. The plate shown in Fig. 69 is a specimen of the dessert service executed by command of our late Queen Victoria, for presentation to the Emperor Nicholas I. of Russia. The commission for this service was given to Messrs. Daniell in 1845,* and it was exhibited with several other rich " dress services " in the Exhibition of 1851. With its deep border of Mazarine blue and the various orders of the Russian Empire enamelled in reserved white compartments, its ugly gadrooned edge and rich gilding, it forms a typical example of the services produced during the first half of the nineteenth century, not only at Coalport, but as we have already seen, to an even greater extent at the Worcester factories. The coloured illustration on Plate XXI. shows the tint of the rose-du-Barri obtained at Coalport. This piece is also probably one of those exhibited in 1851, but the best that can be said for it is that the tint of rose-du-Barri has never been surpassed on English porcelain. It would be difficult to find a more perfect example of the inartistic use of fine material and careful workmanship in the productions of an English factory, even during the first half of the nineteenth century.

---

* The piece is marked in gold, " A. B. & R. P. Daniell, 120, Bond Street & 18, Wigmore Street."

PLATE XXI.

COALPORT PORCELAIN.

Dessert Plate,

WITH GROUND OF ROSE-DU-BARRI, RICH GILDING, AND SPRAYS
PAINTED IN ENAMEL COLOURS.

Shown in the Exhibition of 1851.

Victoria and Albert Museum. From the Jermyn Street Collection.

(*See pp.* 149-150.)

We have already referred to the use of forged marks on Coalport pieces ; commoner pieces were generally unmarked in the early days of the factory, but an early mark is the word " Coalport." On later pieces various marks are found—" *Coalport*," " JOHN ROSE & CO., COLEBROOKDALE." " C.B.D.," also for Coalbrookdale, near which the factory is situated, and this was sometimes contracted to " C.D.," or the same two letters written together. The mark denoting " Felspar porcelain " has already been mentioned, and the connection with Daniells, the London dealers, accounts for such marks as that on the plate, Fig. 69, and for the name " DANIELL, LONDON " on a garter enclosing the initials "C.B.D." Finally, on some few pieces a mark has been found which at first sight may be mistaken for the contraction " & " ; on closer examination it will be seen that this mark is composed of the letters " C " and " S " written together, standing for " Coalport, Salop"; and in the bows are the small written letters " *C*." " *S*." and " *N*," denoting respectively Caughley, Swansea, and Nantgarw, the factories which were all absorbed by the Coalport firm.

CHAPTER XIV.

THE MINOR EIGHTEENTH CENTURY FACTORIES.

STOURBRIDGE, MUSSELBURGH, LOWESTOFT, LIVERPOOL, CHURCH GRESLEY.

IN the previous chapters the history of all the important eighteenth century factories where the processes and methods of English porcelain were developed has been recounted in considerable detail. In order to complete it, a few factories which seem to have been cut off from the main stream of our history, and the productions of which never reached any pitch of artistic excellence, or added anything to the stock of technical knowledge, must be briefly dealt with.

More than twenty years ago Mr. Nightingale reprinted an advertisement from the *Public Advertiser* of May, 1757,* in which the stock of Thomas Williams, a dealer of " Marybone " Street, Golden Square, was offered for sale. It is described as containing an " Assortment of all the Porcelain Manufactories in England, of any account, the largest variety of the Derby or Second Dresden, with Chelsea, Worcester, Bow, Langton Hall, Birmingham, etc." All the factories mentioned are well known with the exception of the one at Birmingham. Nothing is known of this factory or of its wares, and it has been doubted if a porcelain works ever existed in the district. In Dr. Pococke's travels, already mentioned in the account of the Bristol factories, there is a passage which seems to show that before 1750 there had been a porcelain works at Stourbridge, employed in making articles for

---

* *Opus cit.*, fols. lxiv., lxv.

the London dealers. The passage is as follows * : " We came to Sturbridge, famous for its glass manufactures . . . they had also a manufacture of china, with a contract to sell it only to the promoters of it in London ; but on inquiry I found it not carried on."

Stourbridge is in the district of which Birmingham has long been the commercial centre, and it is very probable that the wares described as Birmingham in the advertisement of 1757 were produced at this works. As the business had apparently been worked in conjunction with a glass-house, we may naturally surmise that the porcelain was an artificial glassy porcelain of the French type, and, indeed, its manufacture may have been introduced by foreign workmen, as the Stourbridge glass industry itself was. These two detached fragments of information are all we possess, and unless by a fortunate accident some pieces should be unearthed with a distinctive mark, we shall probably know no more of the Stourbridge or Birmingham porcelain.

Mr. Chaffers long ago drew attention to a statement in the *London Chronicle* of 1755 : " Yesterday four persons well skilled in the making British china were engaged for Scotland, where a new porcelain manufactory is going to be established in the manner of that now carried on at Chelsea, Stratford, and Bow," and also to the statement in a newspaper of December, 28th, 1764 : " We hear from Edinburgh that some gentlemen are about to establish a porcelain manufacture in Scotland, and have already wrote up to London to engage proper persons to carry it on."

Nothing has hitherto been known of any factory or factories in Scotland during the eighteenth century, but while these pages were in preparation, Mr. R. L. Hobson has had the good fortune to discover among the collection in the Museum of Science and Art, Edinburgh, two pieces traditionally ascribed to a factory at Musselburgh, and said to have been made about 1770. The pieces are two quart tankards of common glassy porcelain, resembling in body

* Pococke's " Travels in England, 1750-1751." Camden Society, Vol. I., p. 222.

and glaze pieces of inferior Chelsea porcelain. The glaze has a
very glassy appearance, and is much " crazed." On the front
is a panel with the Dalrymple crest and motto, and under the handle
is the inscription " Over Hailes." The tankards are, in addition,
decorated with sprays of enamelled flowers in the Chelsea style,
but of indifferent execution. " Over Hailes " is identified with
" New Hailes," near Musselburgh, and it seems almost certain
from the existence of these pieces that works existed here, possibly
with the encouragement of some member of the Dalrymple family.
It is probable that this discovery will lead to the identification of
other pieces, and in this way we may learn something of a hitherto
unknown factory. It is, of course, impossible that the factory
can have been of any size or importance, otherwise we should have
known more of its doings, but it will always be of interest as the
first porcelain works in Scotland.

LOWESTOFT.

More controversy has been expended on the productions of
Lowestoft than on those of any other half-dozen factories.
Fine Chinese porcelain, painted in China with European armorial
bearings, has been most unwarrantably attributed to it, and
had one-half of the so-called Lowestoft pieces been made there,
the factory would have been one of the largest and most
important in the whole of Europe. It is really amazing that
from mistaken motives of so-called " patriotism " many writers
should have assigned to a works that had no influence whatever
on the development of English porcelain, pieces which had
obviously neither been made nor even decorated in Europe
at all.

The first attempts at pottery making at Lowestoft seem to have
been in the direction of some form of earthenware, probably a
rough imitation of Delft ware. Gillingham, in his history of
Lowestoft, written in 1790, states that Mr. Hewlin Luson, of Gunton
Hall, near Lowestoft, discovered some clay on his estate, which,
on trial at one of the London china factories, produced a ware

finer than Delft ware. Mr. Luson then set up experimental kilns, and obtaining workmen from London, attempted to make porcelain ; the workmen, however, had been bribed by their former employers and spoilt the pieces. Notwithstanding this discouragement, works were started in 1757 at Lowestoft by Messrs. Gillingwater, Brown, Aldred, and Rickman ; they experienced the same difficulty with rascally workmen, who nearly ruined their venture, but, detecting the plot in time, they were able to circumvent it. This abstract of an account written some thirty years or more after the events by a man who had no practical knowledge of the business, probably means no more than that the difficulties inseparable from the founding of a new manufacture were experienced at Lowestoft as elsewhere. In 1770 the firm was Robert Browne and Co., and they had a warehouse in London, known as the "Lowestoft China Warehouse," at 4, Great St. Thomas the Apostle, Queen Street, Cheapside. From 1770 to 1802-3 the firm seems to have carried on the production of a common artificial porcelain, apparently composed of pipe-clay and glass, until the growing competition of the cheaper bone porcelain made in Staffordshire crippled their trade and caused the partners, who were advanced in years, to abandon the undertaking. Fortunately, we have quite a large number of pieces, bearing names, dates, and inscriptions, which prove the nature and style of the real Lowestoft productions. The small inkstand (Fig. 70) with the inscription in underglaze blue, " A trifle from Lowestoft," will serve to show the style of many of these pieces. Mugs of various sizes, tea services, punch-bowls and dishes seem to have been largely made. They are generally painted with simple designs in underglaze blue, though a few pieces are known in which black has been used. At a late period, probably after 1790, decoration in enamel colours was used, and many pieces are known with roses both in sprays and in festoons, and simple scale and chequer work patterns used as borders. It is stated that printed patterns were used at Lowestoft, but very few pieces of printed ware have ever been found that could by any possibility be ascribed to that factory.

The ware of the authenticated pieces resembles some of the inferior pieces of Chelsea or Bow. It is not very translucent, and has a distinct yellowish tinge when viewed by transmitted light. The glaze was slightly " blued " with cobalt, and is often imperfectly fired, so that it has a dullish look ; it is also very often " specked " with black points, due to careless or imperfect firing.

As an example of the difficulties that have been started with regard to the productions of Lowestoft, we illustrate in Fig. 71 a well-known teapot in the Victoria and Albert Museum. This piece is marked under the foot in red, "Allen Lowestoft." There was a Robert Allen who was one of the first boys employed at the Lowestoft works and afterwards became foreman decorator there. At the close of the works he commenced to deal in pottery, and set up a little kiln, where he fired pieces of his own decoration. In 1819 he is said to have painted the east window of the parish church of Lowestoft with a representation of the Crucifixion. Because this teapot has a painting of the Crucifixion, and is marked " Allen Lowestoft," it has been boldly claimed as a piece from the factory. In reality it is a piece of common Chinese porcelain, rudely painted in on-glaze colours by a Chinese pot-painter, from some European engraving of the Crucifixion. It is well known that the Jesuit missionaries, in their attempts to introduce Christianity into the Chinese Empire, had religious pictures of this kind painted on pieces of Chinese porcelain by native painters. In the late Mr. Cosmo Monkhouse's work on Chinese porcelain * an illustration will be found (Fig. 46) of a Chinese plate with a painting which is identical with that on this teapot.

No mark appears to have been used on the Lowestoft porcelain.

LIVERPOOL.

Attempts have been made to establish the reputation of Liverpool as a porcelain-making centre during the latter half of the eighteenth century, but there is no doubt that in this case, too, a

* Cosmo Monkhouse: "A History and Description of Chinese Porcelain." Cassell & Co., 1901.

FIG. 70.—INKSTAND, PAINTED
IN BLUE.
LOWESTOFT.

FIG. 71.—TEAPOT, MARKED IN RED.
"ALLEN LOWESTOFT."

great deal more has been made of the case than is warranted by any ascertained facts. It is well known that a number of potters were at work in Liverpool during this period, and several of them are said to have made porcelain. Those generally described as " china makers " are Richard Chaffers, who died in 1765 ; Philip Christian, who was Chaffers' executor, and is said to have been the largest potter in Liverpool after the death of Chaffers; and Seth Pennington, of Shaw's Brow.

So little is known of the Liverpool porcelain owing to the absence of marks, and probably also to the fact that much of it was exported to America, that we are compelled to take many statements on trust. We know that Chaffers secured a long lease of a mine of soapy rock, near Mullion in Cornwall, in 1756, and that Christian sold the unexpired portion of the lease in 1776 to the Worcester Porcelain Company. But it has perhaps too rashly been assumed, because soap-stone was used at Worcester in porcelain making, that Chaffers, and Christian after him, must have used it for the same purpose. Sadler, the printer, who doubtless had the most intimate relations with these potters, as he printed their pottery, has left in one of his notebooks a receipt, dated January, 1769, for what he calls " Christian's China Body." This receipt runs : " 100 parts of rock [*soapy rock ?*], 24 parts flint, 6 parts best flint glass, 6 parts crown glass ; to every 20 lbs. of the above 1 lb. of salts." If this was the real receipt for Christian's body, it was presumably closely related to that of Chaffers, who first introduced the use of soapy rock at Liverpool. The point is that the ware produced from such a mixture would not be translucent, and could only have obtained the name of " china ware " from its whiteness, as compared with the general earthenwares of Staffordshire.

In the same notebook of Sadler's there occurs another receipt for a china body : " Pennington's body," dated March, 1769. " Bone ashes, 60 lbs. ; Lynn sand, 40 lbs. ; flint, 35 lbs., fritted together ; to every 60 lbs. of the above, 20 lbs. of clay." The kind of clay is not specified, but in all probability pipeclay would be used for the purpose. This mixture would produce a barely translucent ware, and it is possible that some such "body" may have been used in the manufacture of such porcelain as was made in Liverpool. The Pennington furnishing this receipt was probably Seth Pennington, who had a works among the colony of potters on Shaw's Brow, where both Chaffers and Christian had their works also. He is supposed to have carried on business from 1760 to 1790. A few pieces are known inscribed with a capital P, which is said to have been his mark.

The best known pieces that can with any likelihood be attributed to any of the three Liverpool potters named are bell-shaped and barrel-shaped mugs of various sizes, generally bearing designs printed by Sadler and Green in enamel black. The majority of these are evidently commemorative mugs like those issued from Worcester. A typical piece of this kind is in the Schreiber collection with a portrait of General Wolfe and a trophy of flags and the like. There is in existence also a quart mug, which has among its ornaments a representation of the heraldic "Liver" and the words "Frederick Heinzelman—Liverpool, 1799."

In the nineteenth century porcelain was made for a considerable time at the "Herculaneum" factory, 1800–1841. These productions are generally marked "Herculaneum," or, after 1822, "Herculaneum Pottery," either impressed in the paste or printed. After 1833 the "Liver," the crest of the borough of Liverpool, was often impressed in the paste. The ware produced at the "Herculaneum" factory was so similar to the contemporary Staffordshire production that it needs no extended notice here

CHURCH GRESLEY.

At Church Gresley, near to Burton-on-Trent, but in the county of Derbyshire, a porcelain factory was started in 1795 by Sir Nigel Gresley, close to his residence at Gresley Hall. The Gresley family had long been connected with the Potteries district of Staffordshire, as they were Lords of the Manor of Burslem, and had a seat at Knipersley Hall, in the north of the county. The workmen, who were brought from the Staffordshire Potteries, are hardly likely to have had much acquaintance with porcelain making, but in June, 1795, W. T. Coffee, the modeller, who has been mentioned in the account of the Derby factory, was engaged here. It appears, from a letter written by Coffee, that a Mr. Adderley, another landowner in the neighbourhood, was also interested in the venture. It is probable that the works was carried on in an amateurish fashion, as the young ladies of the Gresley family are said to have painted on the porcelain. The proprietors are also said to have spared no expense in procuring artists to decorate the productions, but, if so, we have nothing to show that was worthy of such expenditure and no real success could have been achieved, for in 1800 the business was sold to Mr. William Nadin, a colliery proprietor living in the district. Nadin carried on the works for four or five years, when it was transferred to Mr. Burton, of Linton, Derbyshire, only to be entirely abandoned in 1808. Jewitt states that one speciality of the factory was the production of fancy pieces in the shape of boots, shoes, and slippers ; while we also read of tea services decorated with paintings of trees in underglaze blue, with carefully painted birds upon the branches, but such pieces are unknown nowadays. It is stated that when Nadin carried on the works he received an order from Queen Charlotte, through Colonel Desborough, her Deputy Chamberlain, for the handsomest dinner service he could make, and the price agreed upon was £700. The order was, however, never executed, as the workmen did not know how to manage the firing of the porcelain, and pieces of any size, when taken from the ovens, were found to be warped and distorted out of all serviceable shape. Such pieces as are now attributed to this factory have a general resemblance to inferior Derby porcelain of the same period, but it is impossible to speak with any certainty of the productions of a factory that, in spite of considerable expenditure, seems to have been a failure from the outset.

CHAPTER XV.

IN the preceding chapters we have been able to trace the history of the important factories of the eighteenth century, and of the three of them—Worcester, Derby, and Coalport—that continued well into the nineteenth century. We have seen how the necessities of practical manufacture led to the supersession of glassy porcelains by more manageable mixtures made from bone-ash, china clay, and china stone ; but it was hardly to be expected that the peculiar beauties of the glassy porcelains should be abandoned without a struggle. The directors of large businesses could not, of course, be expected to engage in such a doubtful enterprise, but a few men who had been trained as porcelain painters evidently appreciated the qualities of the older material so highly that they were prepared to risk all they had, of health, strength, and money, in the effort to re-establish a manufacture of glassy porcelain like old Chelsea or old Sèvres. The best known of these men was William Billingsley, who has already been mentioned in the account of the Derby factory. Great attention has been paid to his doings, but most writers have absurdly overrated his abilities. He seems to have been a restless, ingenious, and inordinately ambitious workman, with a hasty disposition, who might have done something could he have been controlled and wisely encouraged; but he was intractable, and the Fates were unkind, so that his whole history, from the time he left the position of chief flower-painter at Derby, was nothing but a succession of failures—technically, artistically, and financially. During the time that Billingsley worked at Derby—from 1785, when, at the age of sixteen, he was apprenticed to the elder Duesbury, to 1796, when he left the works—he must have come into intimate contact with such of the old Chelsea workmen as had removed to Derby. One of these men was Zachariah Boreman, the landscape painter, and it is asserted that he and Billingsley had a kiln in the house where one of them resided, and made 'experiments together, either in painting or in making porcelain.* It is probable that Boreman had infected the younger painter with a passion for the glassy porcelain of early Chelsea production, and with such information as he possessed, possibly, indeed, with the actual receipt itself, they set themselves to work to reproduce it. Boreman left Derby in 1794, returning to London to work as an enameller for the trade ; and Billingsley left Derby in 1796 to commence the manufacture of porcelain at Pinxton, in partnership with a Mr. John Coke. He left Pinxton in 1801, and began to decorate porcelain (brought from the Staffordshire factories) at Belvedere Street, Mansfield, Notts. This venture was abandoned in a year or two, and he next appears at Torksey, about seven miles from Gainsborough. In a deed dated October 25th, 1805, he is described as "of Torksey, china manufacturer," but it is most likely that his business here, as at Mansfield, was a "decorating" business only. We next hear of him at Worcester, where he worked for Flight and Barr at his old occupation of flower painting from 1808 to 1811, along with a companion, Samuel Walker, who afterwards married his eldest daughter. Here he was apparently in hiding (fearing prosecution for debt or fraud), and passing under the name of Beeley.† Walker, his son-in-law, introduced an improved enamel kiln at Worcester, more like those used at the present time than the clumsy and inefficient box kilns previously used ; and it is stated that Billingsley went over to Coalport in 1811 to erect one of these new kilns there.

In the latter part of 1811 Billingsley and his son-in-law, Walker, broke their engagement with Flight and Barr, and removed them-

---

* Haslem's " Old Derby China Factory," p. 50.
† It is said on questionable authority that after leaving Torksey he started a factory at Wirksworth.

L

selves to a hamlet called Nantgarw, about eight miles north of Cardiff. Here they established a little factory and attempted to manufacture the special porcelain which seems to have been Billingsley's passion. They were at work at Nantgarw in 1812, and by 1814 had exhausted their own little stock of money as well as a larger sum obtained from a Wm. Weston Young, who had joined them. The three men petitioned the Board of Trade for assistance in 1814, but, of course, did not obtain any, and in the same year they removed to Swansea to introduce their porcelain at the Cambrian pottery works there. Billingsley and Walker were as unsuccessful here as elsewhere, and returned to Nantgarw in 1817, but finally removed to Coalport in 1819. Mr. Rose tried their receipt, as we have seen, but soon abandoned it as impractical. Billingsley worked at Coalport as a flower painter till his death in 1828, and it is said that Walker afterwards went to America.

It is evident that Billingsley, who had spent the greater part of his life as a flower painter, had insufficient knowledge or experience to warrant him in setting up as a manufacturer. Even as a mere experimenter he seems to have been unable to learn from his repeated failures. Many formulæ are in existence which are supposed to represent the various mixtures with which he worked, but nothing of a really practical nature has ever been published, and it is only too probable that he worked on no settled plan, but tried mixtures of all the likely and unlikely substances almost at random. He apparently searched for the whitest and most transparent of glassy porcelains—a substance notoriously difficult to manufacture even in the most skilful hands, and demanding greater knowledge for its successful fabrication than he could be expected to possess. We must now turn from Billingsley himself to describe the productions of the three factories where he tried to work out his ideas.

PINXTON.

Pinxton is situated near Alfreton, on the eastern side of Derbyshire, and here Billingsley, with a Mr. John Coke to finance him, first made his porcelain on a small scale. Billingsley left in 1801,

PLATE XXII.

PINXTON PORCELAIN.

Sauce Tureen and Cover.

DECORATED WITH ENAMEL SPRAYS AND GILDING AFTER A WELL-
KNOWN DERBY PATTERN.

(*See p.* 163.)

NANTGARW PORCELAIN.

Plate,

WITH TURQUOISE BORDER AND SPRAYS OF ROSES IN ENAMEL
COLOURS.

British Museum.

(*See p.* 165.)

Mr. Coke sold the concern to a Mr. Cutts in 1804, and the works were finally abandoned in 1812. The authenticated examples are of varying degrees of merit. Some pieces are known, like the tureen illustrated on Plate XXII., and the two large ice-pails in the Victoria and Albert Museum, which are of excellent body and glaze, and well shaped and painted. The majority of the specimens, however, are not nearly so good as these ; they are often almost, if not quite, opaque, badly potted, imperfectly fired, and very slightly decorated. It is generally supposed that the best pieces are those made in the early years of the factory, under Billingsley's management. Several of the painters came from the Derby works, so that it is not surprising to find a general resemblance between the pieces of the two factories, except that the early ware is more transparent than that of Derby. Slight sprig patterns were frequently used for decoration, as at Derby, and the only ground colour used at Pinxton appears to have been the canary yellow for which Derby was so famous. Gold was not lavishly used, and where at other factories the edges and knobs of pieces would have been lined with gold, here they were generally lined with blue or red. The favourite method of ornamenting the ware seems to have been to paint landscapes upon it, the name of the view being written on the bottom of the piece. These landscapes are often in monochrome, and they are generally painted in a very slight and hasty manner, and compare unfavourably with the earlier work at Derby.

Much of the Pinxton ware is unmarked. A " P," written in red over the glaze, is sometimes found, and Jewitt mentions a teapot with the word " Pinxton " written in gold inside the lid.

NANTGARW.

The history of the little factory at Nantgarw is divisible into three periods—1811 or 1812 to 1814, before Billingsley, Walker, and Young went to Swansea ; 1817 to 1819, when they were again at Nantgarw, and before Billingsley and Walker left for Coalport ; and 1819 to 1822, when the works was carried on by W. W. Young alone, with Thomas Pardoe as manager. Young exhausted his resources, and the works was abandoned as a porcelain works in 1822.

The porcelain produced during the first two periods is noted for its transparency, which is greater than that of any other English porcelain,* and for its soft and luscious appearance. Of the ware made during the last period—1819 to 1822—we have no knowledge, as it does not seem to have been identified ; so that in speaking of Nantgarw porcelain one always refers to the ware produced during the two first periods. Collectors have shown the greatest interest in this porcelain, and, attaching undue importance to its transparency and whiteness and to the extremely mannered flower painting upon it, have given it much more attention than it deserves. The fact that a substance is difficult to make adds nothing to its artistic quality ; and those writers who have described this porcelain as superior to Bow, Chelsea, or early Worcester—only comparable, indeed, to the finest Vieux Sèvres—are guilty of exaggeration. From an artistic point of view it is too white, too cold, too much like opaque glass, and lacks the soft and subtle charm of mellow warmth possessed by the older glassy porcelains. It is certain, however, that it was as much admired at the date of its production as it has been in later times, and, could it have been manufactured with any certainty, there is no doubt that a great business would have grown up at Nantgarw. Mortlock, the famous London dealer, was apparently prepared to buy all he could get in the white, in order that he might have it painted in London, and very few painters were employed at Nantgarw besides Billingsley and Young. The best known of these were Latham and Pegg. Pegg came from Derby in 1817, and both he and Latham left the works in 1819. All these men were flower painters, so that the distinguishing feature of the decoration on Nantgarw pieces takes the form of elaborate paintings of flowers and fruit. The same style of decoration was used in London by the various painters

* Of course the porcelain made by Billingsley and Walker at Swansea is the same as this, and appears to have been generally marked "Nantgarw."

FIG. 72.—DESSERT PLATE.
NANTGARW.

employed by Mortlock, though their work was more directly in the manner of Sèvres; and it is probable that the greater number of existing pieces of Nantgarw porcelain were not decorated at the factory but in London.* Plates and tea ware seem to have formed the staple productions of the works, and very few vases or other difficult pieces were made. We illustrate two characteristic plates of Nantgarw manufacture—one from the British Museum, (Plate XXII.), and the other from the Victoria and Albert Museum (Fig. 72).

The general factory marks are the word "NANTGARW." and the same name with the two letters "c. w." (probably for china works) below it, impressed in the paste. It seems probable that the same impressed mark was used on the porcelain made by Billingsley and Walker at Swansea between 1814 and 1817. Owing to the great reputation which the wares of this factory enjoy among collectors, forgery is rife, and the mark "Nantgarw" in red on the glaze is to be regarded with suspicion.

SWANSEA.

When the Nantgarw potters removed to Swansea in 1814, they erected their kilns on land adjoining Dillwyn's Cambrian Works, where earthenware had been made for some years. Dillwyn financed the venture, and when they had been at work for some time, with much loss of ware, he introduced a different and more refractory body. After they left in 1817, a porcelain was made for some years longer, probably down to 1824, by Bevington and Co., who took over Dillwyn's business. There are thus two kinds of Swansea porcelain—the glassy porcelain, exactly like that of Nantgarw (often, indeed, bearing that mark), and a duller, harder, and less translucent ware, which sometimes possesses a distinctly green tinge when held up to the light. This second body is said to have been hardened by the addition of soap-stone, and, when fractured, it presents a closer grain than the granular china of the first period.

* The plate in the British Museum shown in Plate XXII. was almost certainly painted in London.

The later porcelain of Bevingtons' is distinguished by the use of a peculiarly dead-white glaze.*

The Swansea porcelain seems to have been decorated with flower painting almost as much as the Nantgarw ware, but many artists were employed who never worked at the earlier factory. Among these, Pollard, Morris, and De Junic (a Frenchman) may be mentioned; while Baxter, a figure painter from Worcester, also worked here for a short time. In addition to flower and bird painting, decorative scroll work was sometimes used, as in the bowl from the Jermyn Street collection, illustrated in Fig. 74. Another distinctive feature of the Swansea pieces is that ornamental borders modelled in low relief are often found, especially on the rims of plates, and the piece shown in Fig. 72, though marked "Nantgarw," is probably one of those made at Swansea. Modelled pieces, with raised flowers, were also produced, but in no great quantity. The work of this class is attributed to a man named Goodsby, who came from Derby, so that it is not surprising to find that a certain number of pieces were, as at Derby, produced in "biscuit."

The first distinguishing mark on this porcelain was the word "SWANSEA," impressed in the paste. To this a trident, also impressed, was added in 1817, to mark a supposed improvement in the body. The word "Swansea" is also found, both in Roman and italic letters, in red over the glaze, as well as in brown, in blue and in gold. The names "Dillwyn and Co." and "Bevington and Co." have also been noted.

MADELEY—SALOP.

Between 1830 and 1840 there was a small manufactory at Madeley, near to Coalport, Salop, where a glassy porcelain was manufactured with some success. The originator, and sole proprietor of this venture, was Thomas Martin Randall, who must have known Billingsley, and had almost as varied, though much less adventurous, a career. Randall served his apprenticeship at Caughley as a painter, and left there some time after 1790 for Derby. He

* *See* Turner's "Ceramics of Swansea and Nantgarw," p. 72.

FIG. 73.— CUP AND SAUCER—PAINTED
IN COLOURS, GILT EDGED.
SWANSEA.

FIG. 74.- BASIN—PAINTED IN GREEN
AND GOLD.
SWANSEA.

does not seem to have remained long at Derby, for he was working at Pinxton in the early years of the nineteenth century ; and thence he and another Pinxton painter named Robbins went to London and established a little painting and decorating business, working for the principal London dealers, and decorating ware from various English and Continental factories. The workshop of Robbins and Randall was at Spa Fields, Clerkenwell, and they seem to have fired not only their own painting, but that of many other decorators who were painting in London in the same way. It was here that Mortlock had much of the Nantgarw white ware painted, in patterns after the approved styles of the day. When the supply of Nantgarw ware was cut off by the action of Mr. Rose in taking Billingsley and Walker to Coalport, the trade in decorating white or slightly painted Sèvres pieces with rich and elaborate patterns was developed. The London dealers employed agents in Paris to buy up Sèvres pieces in the white, the entire stock of the old Sèvres artificial porcelain that remained in the white having been sold off from that factory in 1813. Pieces with slight patterns were washed with hydrofluoric acid to remove the on-glaze decoration, and then re-decorated with rich ground colours and elaborate gilding and painting. In this class of work T. M. Randall gained his experience of the decoration of glassy porcelain, and in 1826 he left London and returned to his native district. He may have met Billingsley again here, but, at all events, within a few years he had established the little works at Madeley, where he employed two or three potters and several painters, the best known of whom is still alive in the person of Mr. John Randall, of Madeley, noted for his paintings of falcons and pheasants on the later Coalport wares.

The porcelain made here was of true glassy paste with a rich soft glaze. It is of very open, granular texture, and apparently Randall learnt that in order to fire ware of this class successfully, the ingredients of the body must not be too finely powdered. This body formed a perfect ground for the production of a turquoise, composed like the old Persian turquoise, and as Randall's ideal was the fashionable old Sèvres, he soon established a trade with the London dealers in pieces with rich turquoise ground, gilded scroll work, and panels painted with figures, birds, and flower groups, all in direct imitation of Sèvres. Fig. 75 will give an idea of the general style of his productions. This plaque has never left the Randall family, so that its authenticity is beyond question. The ground of the piece is in turquoise, but, even apart from colour, the style and manner of the piece leave no doubt as to the source of inspiration. It should be said that for many years the turquoise grounds produced by Randall were superior to anything else of the kind made in England.

About the year 1840 T. M. Randall left Madeley and removed to the Staffordshire Potteries. There he resided in a house near to Shelton Church, and although he had a kiln and decorated much old Sèvres, he never seems to have manufactured ware again, though he is said to have been invited by Mr. Herbert Minton to introduce his porcelain at the celebrated factory at Stoke-on-Trent, where nearly every species of pottery has been made at some time or other.

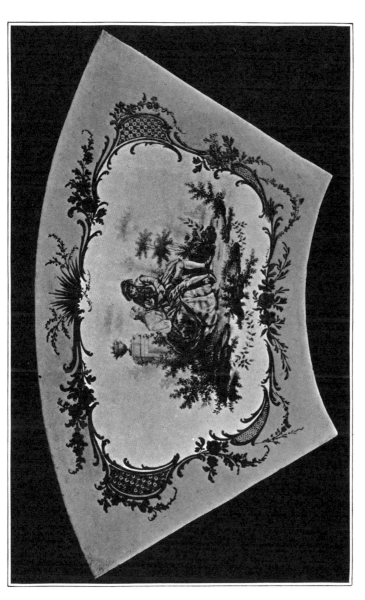

FIG. 75.—PLAQUE FOR TABLE-TOP.
TURQUOISE GROUND AND RICH
GILDING IN THE SÈVRES MANNER.
RANDALL, MADELEY.

CHAPTER XVI.

THE RISE OF THE STAFFORDSHIRE FACTORIES.

THE porcelain factory established at Longton Hall, Staffordshire, about 1752, has been considered at length in a previous chapter, and incidental reference has also been made to the company of Staffordshire potters who purchased Champion's patent rights at the close of the Bristol works in 1781.* This company seems to have commenced business at the existing works of one of the partners, Anthony Keeling, at Tunstall; but disagreements soon arose between them, and in a very short time the business was transferred to the New Hall Works at Shelton. Here it was carried on under the title of Hollins, Warburton and Co., the firm consisting at first of Samuel Hollins, Jacob Warburton, William Clowes, and Charles Bagnall. John Daniell was the manager, and ultimately became one of the partners. Apart from its historical connection with the true porcelain factories at Bristol and at Plymouth, the works is undeserving of notice, as its productions did nothing for the general advancement of porcelain making in England. Very few authentic pieces of its ware are in existence, and the main business of the company appears to have been not so much the making of porcelain as dealing in china clay, ground china stone, and " composition "—a mixture of china stone and limestone—which were all largely used by the Staffordshire potters to improve the quality of their wares. According to the terms of the Act of Parliament extending Champion's rights under Cookworthy's patent, china stone and china clay could not be used in porcelain making without licence until 1796, but a very remunerative trade

* See p. 136.

was done in these materials for earthenware making. It has been stated that the company continued to make true porcelain until 1810 or 1812; but this is very doubtful, as the ordinary Staffordshire processes and the methods of placing and firing were ill adapted to such a manufacture. It matters little when the change to a bone porcelain was made at this works, for its products have no technical or artistic qualities that would render them worthy of attention. The business came to an end in 1825. Two marks are said to have been used at the factory —first an incised " N " in cursive character; and later the name of the factory, " New Hall," in italics, enclosed in a double circle. This mark is generally found printed in a brownish red colour, but marked pieces of any kind are rare.

During the latter half of the eighteenth century the " Stafford-shire Potteries " had attained a commanding position among the pottery centres of Europe by the labours of Whieldon, Wedgwood, Turner, and their contemporaries, and though at first the productions had, for the most part, been confined to various forms of earthenware and stoneware, it is obvious that, with such technical skill and knowledge as had been gradually concentrated in the district, the manufacture of porcelain was certain to be attempted. The great Wedgwood never made anything that has been called porcelain, though among his multifarious productions the " white jasper body " approaches it in translucence, hardness, and beauty of texture; it is, indeed, almost a pedantic distinction to speak of Wedgwood's jasper as " stoneware," and not as " porcelain." Within ten years of the death of Wedgwood, in 1795, the manufacture of porcelain was, however, firmly established in North Staffordshire, and the famous firms of " Minton," " Spode," and " Davenport," so prominent in the history of English porcelain throughout the nineteenth century, were started. In our account of the factories at Worcester, Derby, and Coalport, which, with these three Staffordshire factories, almost monopolised the porcelain industry of England for many years, we have spoken of the general decadence of taste that infected all applied art to a greater or less degree, during the period from 1800 to 1850, so that we cannot expect to find much that was artistically admirable in the work of the Staffordshire factories during the same period. In fact, the art and taste displayed in the ware reached a general level of mediocrity at all the factories, and it is only in respect of the technical qualities of body, glaze, and workmanship that one finds anything to admire in these porcelains.

The rise of the Staffordshire factories may be said to coincide with the final settlement of the composition and processes of manufacture of English bone china. It is most probable that at one of these works—Spode's—the actual transition was made from a body in which, even when bone-ash was used, it was previously fired with some of the other ingredients of the ware, to the mixture of bone-ash, china clay, and china stone,* made without any preliminary fritting, by simply mixing the finely ground materials. It may seem a matter of very small moment to the collector to know how the body and glaze of any particular porcelain was compounded, but historically and technically this change was of the utmost importance, as it at once simplified the process of manufacture, and made the paste or body mixture much more plastic and workable than it had previously been. It must not, of course, be imagined that this new method of procedure, when once discovered, was readily adopted at all the porcelain works; but its advantages were so many and obvious that it has been adopted in almost every works devoted to the production of English porcelain, and within the last thirty years has begun to make headway even in the foreign porcelain factories. In Germany, France, and Sweden bone porcelains made by English methods and processes are now being extensively produced ; while in the United States of America no other form of porcelain appears to have been manufactured. A brief account of the best known factories of the first half of the nineteenth century, apart from those dealt with in previous chapters, may be appropriately introduced here.

* *See* pp. 18 and 19 for approximate composition.

DAVENPORT.

Earthenware factories were started at Longport, a suburb of Burslem, lying down in the valley to the north-west of the town, as early as 1773. About 1793 one of these works passed into the hands of a well-known potter, John Davenport, who, though at first contenting himself with the manufacture of earthenware, developed successively the manufactures of porcelain and glass, which were carried on by him and his descendants down to about 1887. The Davenport porcelain was always noteworthy for good body, glaze, and workmanship, but its decoration was, for the most part, laboured and tasteless, and entirely in the same style as that of contemporary factories. The Prince of Wales (afterwards George IV.) and the Duke of Clarence (afterwards William IV.) visited the works in 1806, and it was probably owing to this circumstance that the service used at the coronation banquet of William IV. was made here. The influence of the Derby factory was naturally paramount with the early Staffordshire porcelain makers, and a close general resemblance between the early Davenport pieces and contemporary Derby ware is perhaps the most striking feature of the productions of this factory. In Fig. 76 is given an illustration of a square *compotier* of Davenport porcelain, formerly in the Jermyn Street Museum, which appears, from its careful and precise workmanship, to be the work of Thomas Steele, one of the Derby painters, who was noted for his painting of fruit pieces. Expensively decorated dessert and tea and coffee services, with rich ground colours, were largely made throughout the history of the factory. Of these ground colours the most distinctive is an " apple green " of peculiar evenness and solidity.

The marks used on the porcelain generally comprise the words " DAVENPORT," and " DAVENPORT, LONGPORT," sometimes alone and sometimes surmounting an anchor. After the manufacture of the royal service for William IV. the crown was occasionally

Fig. 76.—SQUARE COMPOTIER WITH
SCROLL BORDER IN GOLD. FRUIT
CENTRE PAINTED BY STEELE.
DAVENPORT.

used, over the printed legend, "DAVENPORT, LONGPORT, STAFFORD-SHIRE."

MINTON.

Thomas Minton, the founder of the historic firm of "Mintons," was born at Wyle Cop, Shrewsbury, in 1765. We have already seen that he worked at Caughley as an apprentice engraver, and tradition says that he was engaged on the engraving of the first Caughley plate of the "willow pattern." He appears to have left Caughley at the expiration of his apprenticeship, and removed to London to improve himself in the engraver's art. Here he worked for Spode, among others, and this probably determined his removal to Stoke-on-Trent, where he commenced in business as a master engraver about 1789. The process of underglaze blue printing, which had been so largely developed by Turner of Caughley, was then displacing the earlier enamel printing in black on the Staffordshire earthenware; and Thomas Minton, with his knowledge of Caughley patterns and methods, soon built up a business. He engraved the "willow" and "Broseley" patterns of his old factory for the Staffordshire earthenware manufacturers, and by 1793 he appears to have commenced the manufacture of earthenware in a small way on a portion of the site of the present works.

About the end of the eighteenth, or at the very beginning of the nineteenth century, he entered upon the production of china, and this branch of pottery manufacture, the only one with which we are concerned, has been continued on an increasing scale to the present time. It has been generally stated that the first Minton porcelain was only made for about ten or twelve years—down to about 1810, after which it is said to have been abandoned till about 1821. It is impossible to discover any foundation for this statement, and it is believed by those who are now connected with the business, and who are in the best position to know, that porcelain was made continuously throughout the nineteenth century. Thomas Minton, the founder of the works, died in 1836, and the business was continued by his son, Herbert Minton, under whose direction it made the strides that placed it at the head of English pottery firms. The early productions of the factory were not distinguished above those of contemporary factories. A brief sketch of the developments since 1850 will be given in the succeeding chapter.

The mark used on the early Minton china looks like a deliberate imitation of the Sèvres mark. It consisted of two crossed " L's " with a written " M " between them. A later mark is an " ermine spot " in enamel colour or gold. No other marks appear to have been used before 1850.

SPODE.

The largest and most important of the Staffordshire porcelain factories between 1800 and 1850 was that commenced by the Spodes and still continued under the name of " Copelands." The first Spode was a famous Staffordshire potter of the eighteenth century, who produced earthenware and jasper bodies of excellent quality. He died in 1797, and was succeeded by his son, Josiah Spode, who first commenced the manufacture of porcelain, it is said, in 1800. We have already had occasion to refer to this Josiah Spode in connection with the use of bone-ash in the English porcelain body.* Spode was both a good potter and a sound man of business. He neglected no means of improving the quality of his wares, and he certainly enriched the body of his porcelain by adding to it pure felspar, and reducing the proportion of china stone. This alteration made the body richer in tone and quality, uniformly translucent without being too glassy and " thin " looking ; and as his potting was excellent, he soon proved himself a formidable rival of the older factories at Worcester and Derby, where, no doubt, the methods had all become a little old-fashioned and costly. The development of Spode's enterprise was greatly facilitated by the business capacity of his London agent, Mr. Copeland, who became a partner in the concern, with the entire management of the London house. The firm became successively " Spode and Copeland," and then " Spode, Copeland and Son."

* *See* pp. 18 and 171.

FIG. 77.—THREE VASES— CENTRE VASE, GREEN GROUND
WITH RICH GILDING.

SPODE.

In 1826 the elder Copeland died, and in 1827 the second Josiah Spode, the founder of the porcelain manufacture, died also. His son, the third Josiah Spode, died within two years, and in 1833 the entire concern was purchased by W. T. Copeland, commonly known as Alderman Copeland, as he was an alderman of the City of London. He took into partnership his principal traveller, Thomas Garrett, in 1835, and the firm was "Copeland and Garrett" until 1847, when the partnership was dissolved. During the twenty years from 1847 to 1867 the title was "W. T. Copeland, late Spode," and from that date to the present has been "W. T. Copeland and Sons."

Although Spode's porcelain was so well made and of such sound composition in body and glaze, it was not specially distinguished from the artistic point of view. As we have already said, the influence of the Derby productions was felt at all the then Staffordshire factories, and here it appears to have been paramount. We illustrate three Spode vases, which were presented to the Victoria and Albert Museum by Miss Spode, the last direct representative of the Spode family. The centre vase has a dark apple-green ground, and the pattern is painted in solid gold upon it. The vignetted landscapes, heavy forms, and raised "biscuit" flowering of the two side vases are quite typical, and there can be no doubt that Spode had these vases made for himself, as the left-hand one is painted with a view of The Mount, Penkhull, Stoke-on-Trent, where he resided. The fashion set in the Crown-Derby Japan patterns * was quickly taken up by Spode and Copeland, and it seems possible that as much ware decorated in this style was produced at Stoke as at Derby itself. Although many of the patterns are practically copies of those used at Derby, there is plenty of evidence that Spode had before him pieces of genuine Japanese porcelain,† and made some of his adaptations directly

---

* *See* pp. 97–98.

† Among the pieces given to the Victoria and Albert Museum by Miss Spode were several actual Japanese examples.

from them. Spode's productions were superior to those of Bloor's Derby factory in their solid gilding and workmanship, and differed from them in the quality of body and glaze; in other respects it is often difficult to distinguish unmarked pieces of the two factories, so similar are they in style and decoration. The marks of the ware generally correspond to the changes of title of the firm, which are given above. Examples of the best known marks will be found in the section on marks.

WEDGWOOD.

The fact that the great Josiah Wedgwood never made porcelain of any of the kinds dealt with in this book has already been mentioned. In 1805, however, his nephew, Thomas Byerley, who seems to have been most active in the conduct of the business after his death, introduced the manufacture of bone-porcelain. This branch of the business does not seem to have been developed to any great extent, and was discontinued after eight or ten years.* There is nothing to distinguish this ware unless it bears the name. The usual painted landscapes, groups of birds, and flowers with printed outlines, filled in with enamel colour in a quasi-naturalistic style, formed the ordinary method of decoration. A few pieces have been met with having simple conventional flower designs in low relief embossed in the paste; while services and pieces are known with rich gilding similar to that used by Spode.

The mark is the word "WEDGWOOD," generally in red, on the glaze. It has been found in a few instances in underglaze blue and also in gold. Professor Church mentions a dessert service bearing an impressed mark of three human legs conjoined, in addition to the usual mark.

ROCKINGHAM.

To make this sketch complete we must add a brief account of the porcelain factory at Swinton, near Rotherham, in Yorkshire. A factory for the production of common earthenware, of coloured clay, had been started here as early as 1745,

---

* It may be mentioned that the manufacture of porcelain was resumed by the present firm of "Josiah Wedgwood and Sons" about 1872, and is still continued.

Fig. 78.—Saucer—Painted Centre,
Richly Gilded Border.
ROCKINGHAM.

and, as it was situated on land belonging to the Marquis of Rockingham, it was called the " Rockingham " works. This earthenware business was in the hands of a family named Brameld from 1806, and about 1820 they commenced the manufacture of bone-porcelain, obtaining workmen from Derby and the " Staffordshire Potteries." In the commercial panic of 1825-6 they became embarrassed financially, but by the help of Earl Fitzwilliam, their landlord, they were enabled to tide over their difficulties and continued the manufacture of porcelain down to 1842, when, having involved both themselves and Earl Fitzwilliam in heavy pecuniary loss, they gave up business, and sold off the stock, moulds, and implements. It has been stated that this porcelain works was conducted almost regardless of cost, and that the most skilful modellers and painters that could be procured were employed. The first of these statements may be true, for the existing pieces of Rockingham porcelain mark the very perfection of English bone-porcelain in body and glaze. But though the workmanship, whether in potting, painting, or gilding, leaves nothing to be desired, the modellers and painters had no artistic feeling. The pieces were often ugly in shape and over-elaborately decorated, as though the object had been to expend the utmost possible amount of work upon them ; a good instance of this is afforded by the large, ungainly vase in the Victoria and Albert Museum. The dessert service made for William IV. in 1830 was so lavishly decorated that, although £5,000 was paid for 144 plates and 56 larger pieces, its manufacture is said to have involved the firm in heavy loss. All the usual productions of a porcelain factory— vases, figures, jars, dinner, dessert, and tea services, busts, flower baskets, and spill-cups—were made here. We illustrate a piece of fairly simple character in the saucer from the British Museum collection. In addition to the inscriptions " Rockingham Works, Brameld," " Royal Rockingham Works, Brameld," etc., either printed or impressed, the pieces often bear the griffin crest of the Fitzwilliam family. It is said that this crest was not used until after 1826.

M

CHAPTER XVII.

HAVING traced the history of the English porcelain factories and their productions from 1750 to 1850 with considerable fulness, it becomes necessary, in order that our work may be complete, to review briefly the progress that has been made in the latter half of the nineteenth century. During the first half of the century the earlier factories at Worcester and Derby were sinking into decrepitude, and the Staffordshire firms were establishing their position, commercially. The work of this period was infinitely less interesting than that of the first forty or fifty years of our history, and the national stock-taking that followed on the Exhibition of 1851 revealed the depths of banality to which the production and decoration of porcelain had sunk. From about this time, at all events, a decided improvement in taste was shown at the leading factories, and the business of porcelain-making has been conducted with so much enterprise that there are now in England more than seventy factories engaged in this branch of the potter's craft. The majority of these works are, of course, employed in the manufacture of articles having no artistic pretensions, but large and important firms— such as Mintons, Copelands, Worcester, Doultons of Burslem, Brown-Westhead, Moore and Co., the modern Crown-Derby Co., and Josiah Wedgwood and Sons—all produce wares that challenge comparison, in some cases successfully, with the best porcelain of the past. It would clearly be impossible to describe the work of all these firms, nor is it necessary that we should, for the three—Copelands, Mintons, and Worcester—which, along with Coalport, were the only important firms in 1851, have played such

PLATE XXIII.

Minton Vase.

PÂTE-SUR-PÂTE PAINTING, "THE SIREN," BY M. L. SOLON.

Mintons, Limited.

(*See p.* 183.)

a leading part in the modern movement that an account of their principal productions will give the main outlines of what has been done, leaving only one or two minor points to be mentioned separately.

COPELANDS.

As we have seen in the last chapter, the earliest productions of this factory, when it was started by Spode, were noted for the excellence of their workmanship, and throughout the nineteenth century this high standard has been maintained. The bodies and glazes have been of the best, and if the taste displayed in the shapes and decorations has remained very much that of the pre-Victorian period, it can, at all events, claim the merit of historical continuity. It would, indeed, be difficult to point to porcelain in which the solid British taste, on which we sometimes pride ourselves, could show a finer record. French or Japanese art might engage the energies of other factories, but here foreign motives were soon absorbed into the common stock, and furnished only another variation of the ornament that could never have been taken for anything but British. This adherence to the old traditions has doubtless been strengthened by the popularity of the early patterns of the Spode period, for many of these patterns, particularly in Spode's " Old Japan Style," have been continuously made.

It is to this firm that we owe one of the important advances in porcelain-making during the nineteenth century, in the first production of Parian. An account of the composition of this body has been given in Chapter III.,* so that here we need only detail the history of the discovery. Sometime after 1840 a Derby figure-maker named Mountford came to work for the firm of Copeland and Garrett, and, as the reputation of the Derby biscuit figures of the eighteenth century was still very great, experiments were set on foot to re-discover the Derby body. Similar experiments had been made at Derby, as the receipt had been lost, but without success. As pure felspar was used in Spode's china, it was only natural

* *See* p. 20.

that this material should be tried in these experiments, and from this fortuitous combination the Parian body was evolved. At the time of the discovery the credit was claimed by Mr. Garrett; afterwards it was claimed by Mr. Battam, the art director of the works; and when Mountford left the service of the firm he claimed it also. The probability is that, as in so many cases of a similar nature, each of the men contributed to the various ideas that were tried, and each man thought his share the important one. It is very interesting to know of the connection that may exist between the Derby biscuit body, so largely used for figures in the eighteenth century, and Parian, which has been most extensively employed for the same purpose in the nineteenth. The new material is not quite so " waxy " looking as the old—indeed, it resembles a fine statuary marble in quality and translucence. For twenty-five years after its discovery enormous quantities of statuettes, busts, and orna- mental pieces generally were produced, not merely at Copelands, but at nearly every china manufactory in the country. Copelands employed some of the most distinguished English sculptors of the day to model pieces for reproduction in this material, and thus revived an eighteenth-century custom, with the greatest advan- tage. Fig. 80 is a reproduction of a figure of "Narcissus," designed by John Gibson, R.A., and in Figure 3 is a reproduc- tion of a charming group of " Ino and Bacchus," designed by J. H. Foley, R.A.

Many large and important figures and groups were made in Parian, and were extremely popular for a time; but when the pro- ductions of numerous little works had vulgarised the material, it went absolutely out of fashion for this purpose. In the meantime, however, the Parian body had been used as an ordinary porcelain body, glazed and decorated, for the manufacture of all the usual pieces of a porcelain works, and here, too, it has attained a very great success, for when glazed it has a rich, creamy tint ap- proaching that of the old glassy porcelains.

The great International Exhibitions of the last fifty years un- doubtedly fostered the manufacture of large show pieces, in the

Fig. 79.—Vase, and two rich plates.

COPELAND.

FIG. 80.—PARIAN FIGURE. "NARCISSUS."
BY JOHN GIBSON, R.A.
COPELAND.

Fig. 81.—the goldsmiths' vase
(painted by alcock).
COPELAND.

shape of elaborately painted and gilded vases, plateaux, table-centres, and trophies, which, as a general rule, have proved striking examples of the potter's skill rather than of his taste and refinement. Copelands have manufactured many pieces of this kind, such as the large vase, with figure groups painted by C. W. Alcock, which we reproduce. In connection with this department of their work we must mention the names of R. F. Abraham (their art director for many years), who was a well-known figure painter; Hürten, who had a European reputation as a flower painter; and Weaver, who painted bird subjects in a rather stiff and old-fashioned manner. These artists all decorated many large and important pieces.

MINTONS.

We have already spoken of the early days of this factory, and its steady growth during the first half of the nineteenth century. During the latter half of the nineteenth century it occupied for many years the leading position among the porcelain factories of the world. Its high reputation was largely due to the personal efforts of three men—Herbert Minton, who was the proprietor and active manager from 1836 to his death in 1858; Colin Minton Campbell, who succeeded him and remained as business head until 1885; and Léon Arnoux, who came to the works in 1848, and was its technical and artistic director down to 1892.* Mr. Arnoux's first experiments when he came to the works were made in the hope of reviving the manufacture of " true " porcelain in England. The trials were successful, but when the process came to be worked on a large scale it was found that the local materials used for making the " saggers " were not sufficiently refractory, and from this and other difficulties connected with the firing, the experiment was abandoned. Attention was then turned to the improvement of the ordinary bone-porcelain body in use at the works. An excellent body was obtained, quite equal to that of any other English

---

* Léon Arnoux, probably the most distinguished potter of the nineteenth century, passed away at the age of eighty-six, on August 25th, 1902, while these pages were being written.

firm, and with this great developments were made in the porcelain business.

With a Frenchman as director, it was not surprising that many French artists, both modellers and painters, were employed, and the Minton productions during their best period were absolutely French in style and taste. Between 1850 and 1870 sculptors of eminence such as Jeanest, Carrier-Beleuse, and Protat, were successively engaged at the works to design and model figures, groups, vases, centre-pieces, and other works, on a scale such as had only been attempted previously at the various royal or imperial factories of the Continent. Painters such as Lessore, Boullemier, Jahn, Müssil, Pilsbury, and Thomas Allen (most skilful of English figure painters on porcelain), some of whom were the best painters in Europe in their special kind of work, were all employed during the same period in decorating the pieces thus obtained. The great International Exhibitions fostered a demand for these rich and elaborate vases, dishes, dessert plates, and the like, which showed such knowledge and technical skill as had never been brought to bear on any previous English porcelain. Lessore did not remain long at Mintons, but Boullemier, Jahn, Müssil, Allen, and Pilsbury, with many lesser painters, remained for many years, and their productions would need a volume to record them, as they must be numbered by hundreds, if not thousands. The main fault that can be urged against the work of this period is that it is too learned and laboured, and lacks reticence and discrimination. Too often, also, the material has received no consideration, except as something to be painted upon.

The prevailing French taste manifested itself also in a fondness for making copies of some of the most famous pieces of Vieux Sèvres. The special ground colours—turquoise, rose-du-Barri, gros-bleu, and pea-green—of that period were made, and such famous pieces as the " Vaisseau-à-mât," a specimen of which is preserved in the Wallace collection, were copied with admirable fidelity and skill. Chinese porcelain came in for a share of attention, too—indeed, there is hardly a type of fine old porcelain that was not at some time or other imitated at this factory.

FIG. 82.—"AUTUMN." FIGURE IN
PARIAN, MODELLED BY
CARRIER-BELEUSE.
MINTON.

FIG. 83.—VASE IN THE SÈVRES STYLE.
(PAINTED BY HENK).
MINTON.

Fig. 84.—VASES IN THE SÉVRES STYLE
(PAINTED BY BOULLEMIER).

MINTON.

Fig. 85.—PÂTE-SUR-PÂTE PLAQUE BY SOLON.
MINTON.

Most notable of the artistic productions is the work in *pâte-sur-pâte*, introduced in 1870, and still continued by M. L. Solon. The process of painting in clay-upon-clay was developed at Sèvres, where M. Solon first practised it, but undoubtedly it has taken its finest form in his hands. In this process the vessel, which is formed of a porcelain material of the Parian type, is retained in its clay state for a considerable time, while it receives at the hand of the artist a decoration in applied clay. The designs, which in M. Solon's case are almost always figure compositions, are drawn directly on the clay vase, in the mixture of clay and water known technically as "slip." As the vessel is generally shaped in coloured clay—celadon, sage green, dark blue green, rich brown or black—and as white or very slightly tinted slip is used for the painting, it is possible to obtain the most delicate and subtle, as well as the strongest, effects. A thin wash of the slip gives a film so translucent as to resemble only a fleeting cloud on the background; so that by washing on or building up successive layers of slip, by sharpening the drawing with a touch from a modelling tool in one place, or softening and rounding the figure with a wet brush in another, every gradation of tone can be obtained, from the brilliant white of the slip to the full depth of the ground colour. After the first firing a coat of rich glaze of a soft creamy tint is applied, so that the delicate translucence of the material is revealed to the full. Where every part of the process, from the designing of the shapes and ornamental additions to the actual painting, is in the hands of one man, a unity of method and purpose naturally characterises the work. The process is truly that of a potter, and, in the hands of an artist like M. Solon, the results obtained are technically perfect, while, at the same time, with all their strength and technical skill, they combine such delicacy and charm as to entitle them to the post of honour among the artistic porcelains of the nineteenth century.

We are enabled to give two reproductions of M. Solon's work— a vase in colours (Plate XXIII.), and a dish in black and white (Fig. 85). Although we have directed attention mainly to the

more costly and elaborate productions of this factory, the thousand
and one articles of everyday use have also been improved by the
labours of Mintons' artists, and a great variety of patterns has
been produced. Indeed, it is not too much to say that in ordinary
ware Mintons have very largely provided patterns, not only for
some of the smaller makers in our own country, but also for the
foreign pottery firms, who thus endeavour to lessen the debt
which English potters owe to them for past inspirations.

WORCESTER.

In the lengthy chapter devoted to old Worcester we have seen
how the glories of the first factory ended in something very like
eclipse, artistically as well as commercially, between 1840 and
1848. The work of this period had become pitiable, with its childish
painting of landscapes and flower or figure groups, or its hackneyed
repetition of the designs of earlier days, when the factory did
possess spirit and reputation. From this position the works rose
once again to an important place among the English porcelain
firms, and developed certain decorative schemes which have exercised a wide influence on the manufacture both at home and
abroad. Though the sources of these styles have lain in the productions of bygone times and foreign countries their development
has been due to Englishmen, and the work has been carried out in a
characteristically English fashion. It is said that when the factory
was managed by the Barrs in the early part of the nineteenth
century, they were in the habit of telling the workmen that they
wished the work to be regarded not so much as pottery as jewellery,
and this mistaken idea seems to have influenced a great deal of
modern Worcester porcelain, which is marvellous in the fineness
of its detail and the precision of its workmanship, but has the
defects of its qualities, being over-elaborate, fussy, and wanting in
breadth and dignity. One of the first novelties introduced by
the modern firm were vases, ewers, and dishes, in the style of
the later Limoges enamels. These pieces had paintings in white
enamel on the richest of Mazarine blue grounds, and a good

FIG. 86.—PORCELAIN EWER
(PAINTED BY BOTT IN THE
STYLE OF LIMOGES ENAMEL).
WORCESTER, MODERN.

FIG. 87.—ELABORATELY PIERCED PIECES :
WORCESTER, MODERN.

Fɪɢ. 88.—VASE IN JAPANESE STYLE.   Fɪɢ. 89.—VASE IN PERSIAN STYLE.
WORCESTER; MODERN.   **WORCESTER**, MODERN.

idea of their general style may be gathered from the illustration in Fig. 86. It should be said that most, if not all, of the pieces done in this manner, were painted by Thomas Bott, who received all his training at the Worcester works.

The qualities of the Parian body were soon realised by the Worcester firms, and both the Royal Porcelain Co. and Grainger's made good use of this material. Appreciating the creamy quality of the body and its beautiful waxy surface when fully fired in the biscuit state, they took a hint from the wonderful " pierced " work of the Chinese and produced light and elegant pieces, pierced with a skill and dexterity which left the old Worcester piercing (*see* Fig. 41) far behind. Here, of course, the Worcester tradition of patient workmanship proved invaluable. A group of modern pierced pieces will be found in Fig. 87. We have seen how the work of Mintons was largely influenced in its taste and style by French art. The applied art of Japan, which created such a sensation in Europe after the London Exhibition of 1862 and the Paris Exhibition of 1867, had an equally powerful influence at Worcester. There was, however, a difference : in the first case, the French taste was largely followed because the artists were Frenchmen and did what was natural to them ; in the second case, it was the adaptation of an entirely foreign style by men who were highly skilled workmen rather than artists. Bearing these facts in mind, we must give great praise to the Worcester firm for the determination with which they followed their ideals, and for the technical skill which they brought to bear upon every department of the work. With a warm, ivory-like material, which could be treated so as to have a bright or dull finish, and with a variety of coloured golds, they produced a series of remarkable wares, in imitation of Japanese ivories and bronzes. The main fault to be found with this work is that the materials simulated ivory and metal so perfectly that the designers seem to have forgotten that they were working in porcelain. We must, however, admit that this fault is equally shared by the Chinese and Japanese themselves, who never seem

M*

so happy in their work as when they are attempting to make one material look like another. One of the finest examples of Worcester ware in the Japanese style will be found reproduced in Fig. 88. This method became so popular that, once perfected, it has practically remained the basis of most of the sumptuous Worcester pieces down to the present day. Of course, other decorative styles were followed beside the Japanese, and we get so-called Persian, Italian, and Indian wares, but the materials remain the same, and the style, whatever may be its trade name for the moment, has become known all over the world as " Worcester." A piece in what is described as the Persian style is reproduced in Fig. 89.* The making of these elaborate and expensive pieces is only one branch of the many that go to make up a large modern works, and Worcester has been just as famous for its " useful " wares, but to do more than mention these would exceed the limits of our space.

BELLEEK.

As there is only one porcelain works in Ireland, its products may be briefly mentioned here, particularly as they differ slightly in style and manufacture from those of the ordinary English factories. This works is at Belleek, Co. Fermanagh, and is situated on an island where the river Erne leaves the lake of the same name. It was established in consequence of the discovery, about the year 1851, of felspar and china clay in the neighbouring hills. The factory itself was built in 1857, but local materials are no longer used in the porcelain. The body is a Parian of the usual type, glazed with a soft creamy glaze. The one decorative idea of the firm has been to produce pieces modelled in the closest imitation of natural shells and corals, as in the centre-piece shown in Fig. 90. The pieces possess little artistic importance, as the forms are copied with literal accuracy and without any of the " treatment " that an artist would have bestowed upon them. To obtain a still

---

* The rich Worcester pieces here described were generally designed and modelled by Mr. James Hadley and the decoration was executed by James and Thomas Callowhill.

PLATE XXIV.

Group of Flambé Vases.

By Bernard Moore, of Longton.

British Museum.

(*See p.* 187.)

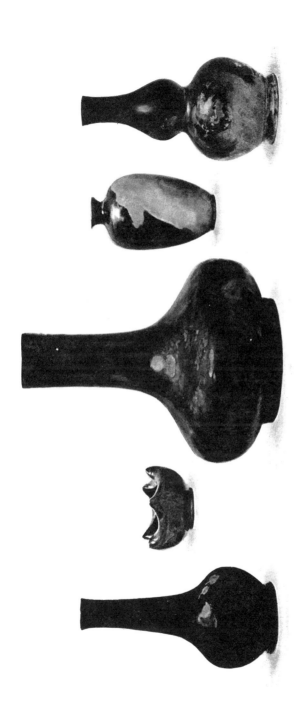

FIG. 90.—PARIAN TABLE-CENTRE.
NAUTILUS AND CORAL.
BELLEEK.

closer resemblance to natural shells, the surface of the ware is usually covered with a pearly iridescent lustre, obtained by firing a film of some bismuth compound upon it, at a low temperature. The effect on the best pieces is singularly delicate and pleasing, but it has been too freely and indiscriminately used to be entirely satisfactory.

ENGLISH FLAMBÉ GLAZES.

The glorious *flambé* glazes of the Chinese have long been the objects of admiration and envy to the potters of Europe. Nearly half a century ago attempts were made in France and in Germany to reproduce them, but for a long time without any success. It was known that the colouring matter of the wonderful ruby, *sang-de-bœuf*, and other varieties of Chinese glaze was an oxide of copper, and that they must be fired in an atmosphere deprived of oxygen to develop the red colour ; but the problem of obtaining satisfactory glazes under such firing conditions proved a most difficult one. Both French and German potters at length succeeded in producing effects in this manner, which, if not identical with the Chinese, were, at all events, worthy of comparison with them. Hardly anyone has known, however, that a Staffordshire potter—Mr. Bernard Moore, of Longton—has been equally successful, and, in addition to producing rich red and *sang-de-bœuf* glazes, has also produced novel and wonderful effects by the use of metals other than copper, treated in the same way. How rich and varied these effects can be is shown in the pieces illustrated on Plate XXIV.* The way in which the colour deepens and lightens over the piece, passing from the faintest grey to the richest brown or vivid ruby red, by imperceptible gradation, recalls the colouring of some piece of precious sardonyx or jasper, and is the final reward of days and nights of labour spent at the potter's kiln.

* Mr. Moore has presented the five pieces here shown to the British Museum.

Glossary.

Armorial china. Services decorated with coats of arms. Much ware of this kind was made in China for Europeans, and whole services have been foolishly attributed to the Lowestoft factory (*q.v.*).

Artificial porcelain. The porcelain which owes its translucence to the large amount of glass entering into its composition. Also called glassy or fritted porcelain (*see* p. 19).

Biscuit ware. In porcelain the paste that has been fired up to the translucent condition before being glazed.

Body or paste. The mixture of materials from which a clay vessel is actually shaped. (For porcelain pastes, *see* pp. 19, 20 and 21.)

Bone-ash. The substance left when bones are calcined. It consists largely of phosphate of lime. Its use is distinctive of porcelain made in the English fashion.

Calcareous clay. An impure clay containing lime.

Can, generally *coffee-can.* A small cylindrical cup, largely made at the Derby factory.

Casting. The method of making porcelain articles by pouring the body mixture in the "slip" condition into moulds of plaster of Paris. The mould absorbs water from the slip, and thus acquires an inner lining of paste. When this has reached the required thickness, the workman pours out the slip that remains liquid, and the mould with its lining of clay is put to dry. The clay hardens and contracts, and can then be removed from the mould.

Cherokee clay. A kind of china clay brought from Carolina, U.S.A., at intervals during the eighteenth century; also called "Unaker."

China. The common English name for porcelain of any description.

China clay, or *Kao-lin.* The purest and whitest form of clay, hence largely used in porcelain making. Chemically, it is a hydrated silicate of alumina. The china clay used in England is obtained from Cornwall and Devonshire, and is sometimes spoken of as Cornish clay (*see* pp. 15 and 19).

China stone, the English equivalent of Chinese pe-tun-tse. It is a pegmatite, consisting mainly of more or less decomposed felspar crystals embedded in glassy quartz. When finely ground it fuses at the heat of the porcelain furnace. It is the fusible constituent in true porcelain, and is also an important constituent of English bone-porcelain (*see* pp. 15 and 19).

Colours. Only a few mineral substances can be used to colour porcelain, on account of the temperature at which they must be fired. They may be used to stain the body or clay material itself, as in the grounds of *pâte-sur-pâte*, or similar substances ; as underglaze colours applied under the glaze and consequently fired up to the temperature at which the glaze itself is fired ; as on-glaze or enamel colours, painted on the glaze after it has been fired, and then re-fired at a lower temperature. Enamel colours always consist of a colour base mixed with a considerable quantity of flux which melts at the enamel-kiln heat and fuses the colour to the glaze. Blue was practically the only underglaze colour used on the eighteenth-century English porcelains. All the other colours and some shades of blue were enamel or on-glaze colours.

Enamel colour. The general term for the colours fired on the glaze (*see* above).

Enamel kiln. The muffle or closed kiln in which the pieces are fired to fuse the enamel colours. It is practically a fire-clay box of large size, which is heated by flues running round it, so that the ware is absolutely protected from flame and smoke. The temperature at which an enamel kiln is fired varies for different purposes. Gold and ordinary painted colours are fired at what is known as "easy kiln fire," about 700°–800° C. Rich grounds which are to receive gilding, such as crimson, maroon, rose-du-Barri, and apple or pea green are fired at a higher temperature, 850°–900° C. This is known as "hard-kiln fire."

Enamelling. In porcelain, the decoration of ware with enamel colours.

Felspar. A double silicate of alumina with one or more of the alkali, or alkaline-earth metals. It is the main ingredient in china stone, and is more fusible than that substance. It is largely used in making Parian (*q.v.*).

Felspathic glaze. A glaze of which felspathic minerals are the chief constituents. The glaze of true porcelain is the felspathic glaze *par excellence*. Many English porcelain glazes have a felspathic basis made more fusible by the addition of borax, soda, and oxide of lead.

Flambé. The mottled and cloudy glazes first produced by the Chinese, but now obtained in Europe by firing glazes containing oxides of copper and other metals in a reducing atmosphere (*see* p. 187).

Flint. A form of silica largely used by potters. Flint pebbles when calcined and ground produce a beautifully white, infusible powder, which is generally preferable to ground sand.

Flowering. The decoration of porcelain with flowers modelled in the round (*see* plates VI. and VII., and Figs. 2, 14 and 64).

Flux. A very fusible glass, rich in borax, oxide of lead, or oxide of bismuth which is added to colouring oxides and to gold to fuse them into the glaze, in the process of enamelling porcelain.

Fracture of porcelains. The appearance presented by the different kinds of porcelain when fractured is often quite characteristic (*see* p. 22).

Frit. The special glass made to give fusibility and transparence to the body of artificial porcelain when fired. The composition of a suitable and unsuitable frit for this purpose will be found on page 10. The term frit is also used to indicate any special glass made by potters for use in glazes.

Fritted porcelain. Porcelain containing frit in the paste (*see* Artificial Porcelain).

Gilding. The decoration of porcelain with metallic gold (*see* pp. 46–47).

Glaze. The vitreous coating of porcelain or pottery generally (*see* also Felspathic Glaze and Lead Glaze).

Glost-oven. The chamber in which the glaze is actually melted on the surface of the ware. The temperature at which this takes place varies with different glazes (*see* pp. 17 and 21).

Grauen, or *Growan*, also moor-stone, the old Cornish name of china stone.

Grauen clay. China clay.

Hard paste. A term formerly used to distinguish true porcelain, because it is generally so hard that it cannot be scratched with a steel tool. It is a very indefinite term and should be abandoned (*see* p. 21).

Indian china. The name generally given to Chinese and Japanese porcelains in the seventeenth and the early part of the eighteenth century, because they were imported by the India Companies of Holland, England, and France.

Ironstone china. A trade name given to a dense form of earthenware largely made in Staffordshire.

Kao-lin. The Chinese name for the mineral substance known in England as china clay.

Kiln (*see* Enamel kiln).

Lead glazes. Glazes which are rendered more easily fusible by the addition of a large proportion of lead oxide. The glazes of the artificial porcelains of Sèvres, Bow, Chelsea, and other eighteenth century factories often contained 40 per cent. of lead oxide. Modern English porcelain glazes contain less than half that amount as a general rule. A few English porcelain glazes are free from lead oxide.

Modelling. The shaping of an original model in clay, wax, etc., by the modeller or sculptor. Casts are taken of this model in plaster of Paris, and copies of these furnish the working moulds in which the pieces of ware are made by pressing or casting.

Moulds. Moulds for porcelain making are generally made in plaster of Paris, as above described. The workman makes the actual piece of porcelain by " pressing " or " casting " (*q.v.*). Intricate pieces are made in parts from separate moulds, and the parts are afterwards joined together by a little liquid slip, until they become united in the firing.

Muffle. An enclosed kiln with the flame conveyed in flues round the outside. The kilns used for firing enamel colours and gold are muffle kiln (*see* Enamel kiln).

Ovens. The larger kilns in which the body and the glaze of porcelain are fired. The flames and smoke pass through the kiln. The ware is enclosed in saggers, but is not so perfectly protected from flame and smoke as in the muffle kilns.

Parian. A special form of porcelain body consisting generally of felspar and china clay (*see* p. 20).

Paste (*see* Body).

Pâte-sur-pâte. The name given to a method of porcelain decoration in which the work is executed in clay slip, while the vessel itself is still unfired (*see* p. 183).

Pegmatite (*see* China stone).

Pe-tun-tse. The Chinese name for the powdered mineral which is used by their porcelain makers, and is equivalent to our china stone. It is the fusible constituent of the body of true porcelain, as well as the principal ingredient in its glaze.

Plateau. A large dish or tray of porcelain.

Pressing. The method of shaping pieces of pottery by pressing thin cakes or " bats " of clay into moulds of plaster of Paris.

Propping. The method of supporting delicate porcelain articles, such as figures, with a scaffolding of pieces of porcelain of the same composition and consistence as the piece itself, so that it shall undergo the firing safely (*see* p. 71).

Refractory. Fire-resisting ; applied to those materials which are most infusible, at the heat of a porcelain furnace.

Sagger. A fire-clay box used to contain and protect pottery during the firing operations.

Siliceous materials. Clays, body mixtures, or glazes rich in silica.

Slip. The thick liquid obtained by mixing clay, or any body-mixture with water.

Slip kiln. A shallow brick-work trough in which mixed slip can be boiled to evaporate the water so as to produce potters' clay.

Soap-stone, or *Steatite.* A silicate of magnesia, which was used instead of silicate of alumina (china clay) in certain eighteenth century porcelains. It was generally obtained from the district near Lizard Point, Cornwall.

Soft paste. A term formerly used to distinguish glassy and bone-porcelains from true porcelain, because they could be readily abraded by a file, while true porcelain could not. With the variety of porcelains now made such a method of distinction is of very little service.

Stilts and Spurs. Pieces of refractory clay with sharp points or edges, used to support articles during the firing of the glaze. Little marks are often found on pieces of ware, where they have rested on such supports.

Throwing: The art of shaping vessels on the potter's wheel.

Unaker. The name given to a china clay brought from Carolina, U.S.A., in the eighteenth century. Also called Cherokee clay.

Underglaze colours (*see* Colours).

Wreathing. The occurrence of spiral or wavy lines in pieces of "thrown" ware, due to imperfect manipulation of the clay. A similar appearance is sometimes found in " cast " ware.

Bibliography.

THE following list of books comprises those that are most useful to students and collectors of English porcelain :—

BEMROSE, WILLIAM.—Bow, Chelsea, and Derby Porcelain. Illustrated. London, 1898.

BINNS, R. W.—A Century of Potting in the City of Worcester. Second Edition. London, 1877.

BINNS, R. W.—Worcester China : A Record of the Work of Forty-five Years, 1852–1897. London, 1897.

BINNS, R. W., and EVANS, E. P.—A Guide through the Worcester Royal Porcelain Works. Worcester, 1898.

BURTON, WILLIAM.—The Influence of Material on Design in Pottery ; Cantor Lectures. London, 1897.

CHAFFERS, WILLIAM.—Marks and Monograms on Pottery and Porcelain. London, 1900.

CHURCH, A. H.—Scientific and Artistic Aspects of Pottery and Porcelain ; Cantor Lectures. London, 1881.

CHURCH, A. H.—English Porcelain : A Handbook to the China made in England during the eighteenth century. London, 1885.

FRANKS, SIR A. W.—Notes on Chelsea Porcelain. "Archæological Journal," 1862.

HASLEM, JOHN.—The Old Derby China Factory. London, 1876.

JEWITT, LLEWELLYN.—The Ceramic Art of Great Britain. Two Vols. London, 1878.

LITCHFIELD, FREDERICK.—Pottery and Porcelain, a Guide to Collectors. London, 1900.

MAYER, JOSEPH.—History of the Art of Pottery in Liverpool. Liverpool, 1855.

NIGHTINGALE, J. E.—Contributions toward the History of Early English Porcelain. Salisbury, 1881.

OWEN, HUGH.—Two Centuries of Ceramic Art in Bristol. Gloucester, 1873.

RANDALL, JOHN.—History of Madeley, including Ironbridge, Coalbrookdale, and Coalport. Madeley, 1880.

REEKS, T., and RUDLER, F. W.—Catalogue of Specimens of English Pottery in the Museum of Practical Geology. Third Edition. London, 1876.

SHAW, SIMEON.—History of the Staffordshire Potteries. Hanley, 1829. Re-issue by " Pottery Gazette." London, 1900.

SHAW, SIMEON.—The Chemistry of Pottery. London, 1837. Re-issue by " Pottery Gazette." London, 1900.

TIFFIN, F. W.—A Chronograph of the Bow, Chelsea, and Derby China Factories. Salisbury, 1875.

TURNER, WILLIAM.—The Ceramics of Swansea and Nantgarw. Illustrated. London, 1897.

PLATE XXV.

Impressed Marks.

INCISED TRIANGLE.   ANCHOR STAMP.

EARLIEST CHELSEA MARKS.

ANCHOR STAMP. (BROKEN.)	ANCHOR STAMP.	ANCHOR STAMP. THE ANCHOR COLOURED.

IMPRESSED B.   IMPRESSED   IMPRESSED   IMPRESSED
SUPPOSED TO INDI-   ARROW   CADUCEUS.   T.
CATE THE WORK   AND
OF JOHN BACON.   ANNULET.

BOW MARKS.

PLATE XXVI.

Impressed Marks.

FLIGHT,
BARR & BARR.

FLIGHT,
BARR & BARR.

BARR,
FLIGHT & BARR.

BARR, FLIGHT
& BARR.

CHAMBERLAINS,
WORCESTER.

MODERN
WORCESTER.

THE MARK ON
SAUCE BOAT.
(FIG. 54).

THE MARK ON
SAUCE BOAT.
(FIG. 55.)

BRISTOL MARK.
SUPPOSED TO BE A
CONTRACTION FOR
TEBO (MODELLER).

NANTGARW.

SWANSEA.

SPODE.

 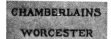

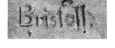 

PLATE XXVII.

Marks Painted in Red (on glaze).

ANCHOR MARKS OF CHELSEA,
SHOWING VARIATIONS IN STYLE AND SIZE.

CHELSEA.   BOW.   BOW.

ANCHOR AND DAGGER MARKS OF BOW,
SHOWING VARIATIONS IN STYLE AND SIZE.

PLATE XXVIII.

Marks Painted and Printed in Red (on glaze).

PAINTED CROWN-DERBY MARKS.
PERIOD, 1782–1810.

PRINTED CROWN-DERBY MARKS.
PERIOD, 1810–1848.

PLATE XXIX.

Marks Painted and Printed in Red (on glaze).

RARE EXAMPLE
OF WORCESTER
CRESCENT MARK.

CHAMBERLAINS.
(WRITTEN.)

CHAMBERLAINS.
(WRITTEN.)

CHAMBERLAINS.
(WRITTEN.)

CHAMBERLAINS.
(WRITTEN.)

CHAMBERLAINS.
(WRITTEN.)

CHAMBERLAINS.
(PRINTED.)

GRAINGER LEE & CO.
(WRITTEN.)

GEORGE GRAINGER.
(WRITTEN.)

Chamberlains
Worcester

Chamberlains
Worcester

Chamberlains
Worcester.

Chamberlain & Co
Worcester
155 New Bond Street
& No 1 Coventry Street
London

Chamberlains
Regent China
Worcester
& 155.
New Bond Street
London.

Grainger Lee & Co
Worcester

George Grainger
Royal China Works
Worcester

PLATE XXX.

Painted and Printed Marks in Red (on glaze).

PLYMOUTH MARKS.

MARK ON
TEAPOT.
(FIG. 71.)

MARK ON
A PINXTON PIECE.
(NAME OF SCENE.)

SWANSEA.
(WRITTEN.)

DAVENPORT.
(PRINTED.)

DAVENPORT.
(PRINTED.)

ROCKINGHAM.
(PRINTED.)

SPODE.
(WRITTEN.)

SPODE.
(WRITTEN.)

SPODE.
(WRITTEN.)

SPODE.
FELSPAR
PORCELAIN.
(PRINTED.)

♃   ♃   2ↄ

Allen
Lowestoft

Near Ingleby.
Derbyshire.
P

Swansea

Davenport
LONGPORT.

DAVENPORT

Rockingham Works.
Bramele.

SPODE   SPODE   Spode

Spode
Filspar
Porcelain

PLATE XXXI.

Marks Painted in Blue (underglaze).

EARLY WORCESTER MARKS.

EARLY WORCESTER MARKS IN IMITATION OF
ORIENTAL SEAL MARKS.

EARLY WORCESTER MARKS.
(SHAM ORIENTAL.)

WORCESTER MARKS, FLIGHT PERIOD (1782–1792).	IMITATION DRESDEN MARK, WORCESTER.	IMITATION SÈVRES MARK, WORCESTER.

CAUGHLEY MARKS.

COALPORT.	IMITATION SÈVRES MARK, COALPORT. (*See* FIG. 68.)	EARLY MINTON MARK.

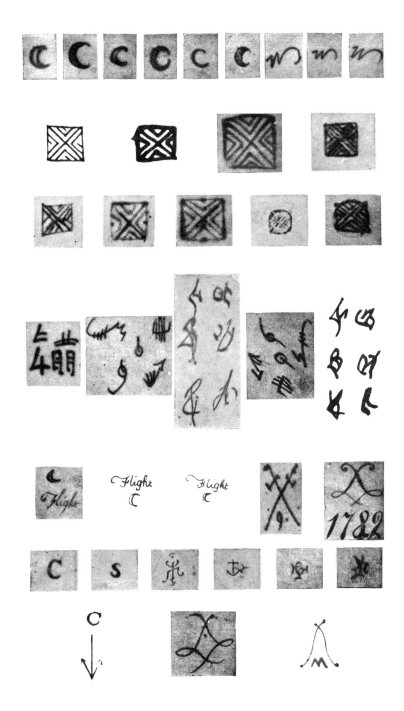

PLATE XXXII.

Marks Painted in Blue (underglaze).

EARLY CROWN-DERBY MARKS.

IMITATION
SÈVRES MARK,
DERBY.

PLYMOUTH MARKS.

PLYMOUTH-
BRISTOL MARK.

IMITATION DRESDEN MARKS,
BRISTOL.

BRISTOL MARKS.

BRISTOL MARKS.
(THE NUMERALS OFTEN OCCUR IN GOLD.)

LONGTON HALL
MARKS.

MONOGRAMS OF T. F.
BOW.

BOW MARKS.

PLATE XXXIII.

A Series of the Gold Anchor Marks of Chelsea.

SHOWING THE VARIATIONS IN SIZE AND STYLE OF THE ACTUAL
MARKS.

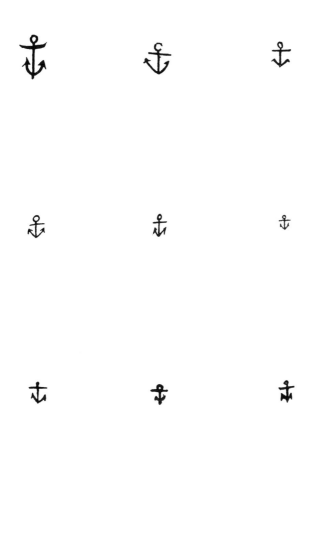

PLATE XXXIV.

Marks Painted in Gold (on glaze).

DERBY-CHELSEA MARKS IN GOLD.

DERBY-CHELSEA MARK.
(THE FLOWER IS IN COLOURS.)

THE MARKS ON THE THREE CUPS AND SAUCERS.
(FIGS. 18, 19, 20.)

RARE EXAMPLE OF   SPODE.

PLYMOUTH MARKS.   WORCESTER CRESCENT   (WRITTEN.)

MARK.

PLATE XXXV.

Marks Painted and Printed in Puce and Green.

CROWN-DERBY MARKS IN PUCE.

CROWN-DERBY MARK
IN PUCE.

RARE CHELSEA MARK
IN PURPLE.

ROCKINGHAM MARK.
(PRINTED.)

ROCKINGHAM MARK.
(PRINTED.)

COALPORT MARK.
(PRINTED.)

CROWN-DERBY MARK
IN GREEN.
(PAINTED.)

COPELAND & GARRETT.
(PRINTED.)

COPELAND & GARRETT.
(PRINTED.)

COPELAND.
(PRINTED.)

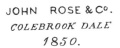

JOHN ROSE & Cᵒ.
COLEBROOK DALE
1850.

INDEX.

PRINTED BY CASSELL & COMPANY, LIMITED, LA BELLE SAUVAGE, LONDON, E.C.